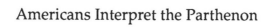

Americans Interpret the Parthenon

Americans Interpret The Parthenon

THE PROGRESSION OF GREEK REVIVAL ARCHITECTURE
FROM THE EAST COAST TO OREGON
1800–1860

Robert K. Sutton

UNIVERSITY PRESS OF COLORADO

9 8 7 6 5 4 3 2 1

The University Press of Colorado is a cooperative publishing enterprise sup-
ported, in part, by Adams State College, Colorado State University, Fort
Lewis College, Mesa State College, Metropolitan State College of Denver,
University of Colorado, University of Northern Colorado, University of
Southern Colorado, and Western State College.

Library of Congress Cataloging-in-Publication Data

Sutton, Robert Kent.
    Americans interpret the Parthenon: the progression of Greek revival
architecture from the East Coast to Oregon, 1800–1860 / Robert K.
Sutton.
        p. cm.
    Includes bibliographical references and index.
    ISBN 0-87081-259-9
    1. Greek revival (Architecture) — United States. 2. Architecture,
Modern — 19th century — United States. 3. Architecture — United
States. I. Title.
NA710.5.G73S88 1992
720'.973'09034 — dc20   92-4077
                                                                    CIP

The paper used in this publication meets the minimum requirements of the
American National Standard for Information Sciences—Permanence of
Paper for Printed Library Materials. ANSI Z39.48–1984

∞

Dedicated to Harriet and Lee David

CONTENTS

ILLUSTRATIONS

PREFACE

Several years ago when I began my career in historic preservation, my first assignment was to compile an inventory of Oregon's historic sites and buildings. I worked my way through file cabinets of clippings, scribbled notes, phone messages, photographs, and letters. It seemed that each time I reached the point at which I could not continue, I encountered houses that were built in the 1850s, were constructed with California gold rush money, and were Greek Revival in style. Eventually I finished assembling the inventory and went on to other things; but I could not forget these houses. My curiosity about them became an obsession that led me to the present investigation. As this project took shape, I wanted to know why Oregonians chose houses in this particular style and how they acquired the tools, technology, and architectural references to build them.

In beginning my study with the architectural literature, I found that early historians charted a clear and comprehensive course through the Greek Revival style. They discussed monumental and vernacular examples, interpreted origins and trends, analyzed the reference sources, and critiqued the architects and builders. On the one hand, though, their studies end at the Missouri River. On the other, historians of the westward movement have written about the politics, economics, societies, and cultures of the West. Few, however, have studied architecture for primary source material.

Buildings are the most tangible evidence of a culture. Whether grand or humble, elaborate or plain, all structures yield information about the builders, the owners, the communities, and the periods in which they were built. What is more, these structures tell their stories in their own language, one which has been codified by architectural historians, cultural geographers, and folklorists. For example, instead of describing the front of a Greek temple by saying it has slender indented columns with scrolls on top that support a triangular-shaped overhang, the language of architecture simply calls this feature an Ionic portico. The term Greek Revival was unknown to Oregon pioneers; the label was created by twentieth-century historians.

The following story tells how a group of pioneers traveled across the plains to Oregon and settled the land. When gold was discovered in California, they hurried there and were among the first to strike it rich. They returned home and used their capital to build new houses. For style, they selected Greek Revival, one with which they were familiar and comfortable.

The present investigation has been an adventure in which many individuals and institutions have participated. First the staff at the Avery Architecture Library at Columbia University graciously opened files collected by Talbot Hamlin and directed me to the rich source materials on Greek Revival architecture in the library. The librarians in the Maps and Photographs Division of the Library of Congress directed me to the Historic American Building Survey. The staff at the Beinicke Rare Books Library at Yale University directed me to a recently acquired collection of letters from Alvin T. Smith and his wife. Librarians at the Huntington Library copied a handwritten autobiography donated by the family of Captain John Ainsworth. Historians at the National Register of Historic Places gave me access to their files and allowed me to copy the Greek Revival nominations. Librarian Louis Flannery and my former associates at the Oregon Historical Society located collections relating to Greek Revival houses, including Alvin T. Smith's diary and the Jameson Parker file of the Historic American Building Survey in Oregon. Manuscript librarian, Layne Woolschlager, located and sent me information on the first Oregon State Capitol. Elizabeth Walton Potter, architectural historian at the Oregon State Historic Preservation Office, searched the files, found photographs of Oregon's classical houses, and expedited having them copied for me. Gregg Olsen shared the valuable insights he gained by restoring several Oregon Greek Revival structures. By duplicating or repairing many features with the actual historical tools, he understood how pioneer builders constructed these houses.

I am greatly indebted to David H. Stratton, who encouraged and pushed me when I needed motivation, praised me when I was on the right track, and offered numerous valuable suggestions. Without Professor Stratton's assistance and proding, the project might well have not been completed. I would also like to thank Edward M. Bennett, John R. Jameson, Henry Matthews, and Peter Iverson for reading various drafts and offering their valuable comments and suggestions. Ms. Jody Berman, my editor, provided a great deal of help through the publication process. The anonymous readers for the University Press of Colorado offered a number of invaluable suggestions as well. Ms.

Sherrie Bridge, my former colleague in Albuquerque, New Mexico, volunteered her time and talent to designing, drawing, and labeling the diagrams in the glossary.

Finally, my wife, Harriet, has been my source of strength. She read the manuscript in its various drafts, made helpful suggestions, and served as a sounding board for many of my ideas during the course of preparing this study. My two-year-old son, Lee David, has been a marvelous inspiration as well.

ROBERT K. SUTTON

Americans Interpret the Parthenon

1

Introduction

Tucked away in the Oregon Historical Society library is an obscure but wonderful manuscript — the diary of Alvin T. Smith. Smith started his daily journal in 1840, just before immigrating to Oregon, and continued it until his death in 1887. Typical entries read as follows: "Feb 12 [1840, Quincy, Illinois] Talked some about going over the rocky mountains. Feb 13 ditto and prayed about it. Feb 14 did the same and concluded to go." Several days later he interviewed and married Miss Abigail Raymond. Then he left for Oregon. When he arrived, he spent a year assisting the Reverend Henry Spalding in building a sawmill at Lapwai, near present-day Lewiston, Idaho. At the conclusion of that project, he went to the Willamette Valley to start an independent mission to the local natives.

Some fourteen years later, Smith's diary included these entries: "Nov 6 [1854] got lumber from sawmill. April 1 [1855] bought 2000 shingles. Aug 10 [1855] worked on house again." Here, he described the process of building his Greek Revival house in Forest Grove (Figure 1.1). In the intervening years, he had settled his land claim, successfully invested in several business ventures, and accumulated a comfortable fortune selling timber and produce during the California gold rush. This new house was the fruit of his labor. He was a skilled carpenter, and with the exception of hiring a local cabinetmaker to craft a fireplace mantle and repair several pesky leaks, he built the entire residence himself in eighteen months.[1]

Smith's house communicates — in a tangible and powerful way — how culture is transmitted from one area to another. His residence is remarkably similar to the New England manifestations of Greek Revival architecture. More specifically, it looks like houses from his hometown of Branford, Connecticut (Figures 1.2–1.5). Although Smith left Connecticut some twenty years earlier, he maintained strong ties to his family there. Also, when Smith left Branford, the best houses in

1

Figure 1.1: Alvin T. Smith House, Forest Grove, Oregon. Built by Alvin T. Smith, 1855. *Courtesy Oregon State Parks.*

the finest neighborhoods were Greek Revival in style. Thus, when he had the means to build a fancy new house, he remembered and copied the most elegant buildings of his hometown. His house gave him a sense of security and attachment to his roots. Although he was perfectly content to remain in Oregon, his house provided the subtle, but constant, reminder of his family and home.

The houses of two other Oregonians further illustrate this selection process. Charles Applegate and Daniel Waldo migrated to Oregon in the 1840s. They were neighbors in Missouri, although Applegate was born in Kentucky and Waldo in Virginia. They came to Oregon as members of the same wagon train, remained close friends in their new homeland, and held similar political views. With this commonality of interests, it would seem logical that they might construct similar dwellings. Such was not the case. Waldo built a Federal style house, with little decoration, that was similar to many residences found in Virginia (Figure 1.6). Applegate's residence was a vernacular representation of the Greek Revival style, which was just coming into vogue when he left Kentucky (Figure 1.7). Both men remembered their childhood homes with affection, and neither cared much for his brief sojourn in Missouri. When they selected models for their new houses,

Figure 1.2: Greek Revival house, Branford Point Historic District, Branford, Connecticut. Unknown builder, ca. 1832. *Courtesy Connecticut Historical Commission.*

Figure 1.3: Greek Revival house, Branford Point Historic District, Branford, Connecticut. Unknown builder, ca. 1833. *Courtesy Connecticut Historical Commission.*

Figure 1.4: Greek Revival house, Branford Point Historic District, Branford, Connecticut. Unknown builder, ca. 1832. *Courtesy Connecticut Historical Commission.*

Figure 1.5: Greek Revival house, Branford Center Historic District, Branford, Connecticut. Unknown builder, ca. 1830. *Courtesy Connecticut Historical Commission*.

Figure 1.6: Daniel Waldo House, Marion County, Oregon. Unknown builder, ca. 1855. *Courtesy Oregon State Parks*.

Figure 1.7: Charles Applegate House, Douglas County, Oregon. Unknown builder, 1855. *Courtesy Oregon State Parks.*

they wanted designs that brought back pleasant memories, rather than the unhappy recollections of the Midwest.[2]

Smith, Waldo, and Applegate built homes based on memories of similar dwellings in their home states, images that remained intact although imprinted many years earlier and several thousand miles away. A non-Oregonian offers a most striking example of how powerful a nostalgic impression can be. Frederick Douglass purchased a house late in his life that looked remarkably like the plantation "big house" of his youth (Figure 1.8). He was born into slavery in 1818 in Talbot County, Maryland, then rented to a ship caulker in Baltimore, from whom he escaped in 1838. He became one of the most articulate and powerful forces in the antislavery movement before the Civil War and one of the most tireless advocates for the rights of blacks after the war. In his 1855 book, *My Bondage and My Freedom,* Douglass recalled the plantation house of his youth:

> The great house was a large, white, wooden building, with wings on three sides of it. In front, a large portico, extending the entire length of the building, and supported by a long range of columns, gave to the whole establishment an air of solemn grandeur. It was a treat to

6

Figure 1.8: Wye Plantation House, Easton vicinity, Maryland. Unknown builder, front portico added ca. 1800. *Courtesy National Park Service.*

my young and gradually opening mind, to behold this elaborate exhibition of wealth, power and vanity.[3]

Some twenty years after he made this statement, Douglass purchased Cedar Hill, a house in Washington, D.C., that sits prominently on the heights of Anacostia overlooking the National Capitol and the city (Figure 1.9). The conclusion is inescapable. Obviously this rare pleasant memory from an otherwise painful youth left an indelible impression on Douglass's mind. When he accumulated the wherewithal to purchase a fine house, he selected one that looked remarkably like the plantation house of his childhood.

Douglass left a rich and voluminous written legacy, but nowhere in his letters, books, or diaries does he suggest the connection between Cedar Hill and the Wye Plantation House. Smith, Applegate, and Waldo as well left no tangible evidence concerning their reasons for design selection. Yet the artifacts — the houses themselves — provide invaluable insights into the reasons for their architectural choices.

Figure 1.9: Cedar Hill (Frederick Douglass House), Anacostia, Washington, D.C., 1859. Purchased by Douglass in 1877. *Courtesy National Park Service.*

Smith's house and a group of some forty other known Greek Revival residences provide a focus for this study. Like the house owners mentioned above, not one gave a reason for selecting the house style. In Anglo-American heritage, however, an individual's dwelling is one's castle. It is the most prized possession and physical evidence that he or she has "succeeded." Because the house is such an important element in American life, there is no better way to analyze the cultural roots of pioneers than to understand how and why they selected particular styles and models for their dwellings. Several factors coalesced at the same time to make Greek Revival houses in Oregon so important. The owners shared many things in common. Most did not make a significant impact on the course of Oregon history. Few of their houses were architectural gems. Many migrated to Oregon during the 1840s. All prospered from the California gold rush — either by making the journey to the diggings themselves or by staying in Oregon and providing goods or services to the miners. Finally, they universally chose the Greek Revival style for their dwellings. These similarities provided the impetus for further investigation.

From this evidence, it might appear that Smith and the others comprised a unique frontier community of philhellenes who read Homer and Aristotle and were on intimate terms with Iktinos's Parthenon. On the contrary, it is highly unlikely that any read Greek or knew about the Parthenon. Further, it is quite clear that they did not use the term Greek Revival to describe their houses. Twentieth-century architectural historians invented this label to identify houses that were built in the early to mid-1800s, and that either resembled classical structures or displayed Greek-like detailing. Architectural styles — unlike substances in the Periodic Table of the Elements — are not absolute definitions. Instead, they are simply descriptive terms to classify buildings, subject to disagreements among architectural historians.

Greek Revival architecture first appeared in Europe in the mid-1700s, inspired by the magnificent volumes prepared by James Stuart, Nicolas Revett, and others, who illustrated the monuments of the ancient world. Stuart was the first to translate his drawings into a building with his Greek Doric Temple in Hagley Garden, England (1758). His creation and the works of his contemporaries that followed set the trends for classical architecture in the Western world. They attempted to capture the spirit of classical architecture rather than making exact copies of entire antiquities. For example, the most commonly reproduced ancient structures — the Monument of Lysicrates (Athens) and the Tower of the Winds (Athens) — were blended into building features such as church towers.[4]

Greek Revival architecture crossed the Atlantic some fifty years later. The first representations — America's high style phase — were, for the most part, created by professional architects who used the materials and sourcebooks of European designers. As a general rule, however, American architects were less concerned with authenticity than their European counterparts. This is not to say that American designers created lesser buildings; their priorities simply did not require a canonical adherence to archeologically correct orders and details.

Close behind the high style period of Greek Revival architecture, the vernacular phase exploded onto the American landscape and spread from coast to coast. Using pattern books and other buildings for guidance, and making use of the handiest or least expensive materials available, designers and builders crafted a remarkable collection of edifices. The style culminated with the Greek Revival houses in Oregon.

One of the classic works in American architectural history, Talbot Hamlin's *Greek Revival Architecture in America* (1944), was the first major volume on the style. Hamlin theorized that Greek Revival architecture was an expression of American genius and a reflection of national spirit. "Never before or since," he wrote, "has there been a period when the general level of excellence was so high in American architecture, when the ideal was so constant and its varying expressions so harmonious . . . as during the forty years from 1820 to the Civil War."[5] Hamlin downplayed European influences on the style, believing that the major components were created at home as evidence of democratic expression.

Hamlin's work has withstood the test of time; it is still in print and widely circulated after nearly fifty years. In fact, it remained as the major national discussion of the Greek Revival style until Roger Kennedy's *Greek Revival America* appeared in 1989. In this magnificently illustrated volume, Kennedy looks more extensively at the social, political, and economic forces that contributed to the style. He, like Hamlin, believed that Greek Revival architecture was a tangible manifestation of independence and nationalism; he departed from his predecessor, however, in his view of the European influences. He argued that Europe directly influenced American stylistic development. European architects migrated to the United States to ply their trade, bringing with them their experience and design handbooks on Greek Revival architecture. Kennedy also devoted much attention to patrons — such as Nicolas Biddle — who influenced the development and popularity of the style.[6]

The books by Hamlin and Kennedy provide thorough discussions of the style east of the Missouri River; however, they do not fully address the spread of the style to the West.[7] The present volume will pay particular attention to the vernacular phase in the West. To begin with, the term vernacular does not imply that the Oregon houses are any less significant than the so-called high style structures that Kennedy and Hamlin discuss. The label simply means that they were designed by carpenters rather than architects, were the homes of common folk such as Smith rather than the landed gentry, and were understated in their design and materials rather than monumental. Also, vernacular structures seldom were documented with written materials. Yet buildings, as primary sources, can speak volumes if one learns to analyze the information they impart.

Architectural historians have developed the language for building styles and components. They, cultural geographers, American studies specialists, art historians, archeologists, preservationists, folklorists, and others have established a variety of methodologies for understanding vernacular structures, producing a remarkably rich and varied body of literature. In each theoretical framework, scholars consistently focus as much on the people who create vernacular architecture as on the structures themselves. In other words, their methodologies are designed to read the information each building communicates about its builders and users, its community, and its historical context.[8]

Cultural geographers and folklorists have developed methodologies to determine the distribution of vernacular buildings and ascertain settlement patterns. They are more interested in the spatial arrangements of structures than with appearances. The folk houses they study are identified by house types rather than architectural styles. For example, a shotgun house is long and narrow, with rooms connected to each other and without a central hall. A dogtrot house has two or four cribs (rooms) that are attached by a common roof but separated with an open breezeway. Thus, geographers are more interested in the shapes and sizes of buildings than with stylistic components.[9]

Once they have gathered a sufficient sample of shotgun houses, geographers group them and plot their disbursement on maps. When there is adequate topographical distribution, the structures collectively demonstrate settlement patterns. Each type is rooted in what Fred Kniffen, the pioneer in the field, calls a "cultural hearth." As pioneers moved west, they created settlement lines or patterns that were attached to an origin. For example, the I-house originated in New England, then moved westward through upper New York and the Great Lakes region into the northern Midwest with few structural variations.[10]

Scholars have analyzed the diffusion of folk housing over the past fifty years. Yet while floor plans tended to remain constant along settlement lines, house styles often changed. Taste dictated variations in the appearance of vernacular dwellings. Further, builders learned the new skills and techniques necessary to create a new style, then incorporated these features into familiar house types. Of the resources available to carpenters, architectural pattern books figured prominently. According to architectural historian Dell Upton, American builders borrowed from these sources selectively, using pieces of plans or details that fit their needs instead of copying entire structures.

11

Pattern books changed the nation's vernacular housing character from distinctive early — and often ethnic — regional folk housing to a more homogeneous national form by the Civil War.[11]

The vernacular architecture of the West presents interesting problems. For instance, during the migration process, Oregonians often lived in two, three, four, or more localities before coming West. These peripatetic pioneers often crossed settlement pattern lines several times, which exposed them to many house types. Thus, the state's building stock included a wide variety of folk housing rather than the predictable types, associated with settlement patterns, identified by cultural geographers. Further, the pattern books that were popular with carpenters in the East and Midwest were not as widely available to Oregon builders. With such a wide range of house types, it would seem that style selection would be equally diverse. Such was not the case. Oregon's architectural trend setters of the 1850s almost exclusively selected Greek Revival style.

This study is an analysis of westward movement using architecture as a vehicle rather than an architectural history using the West as an arena. As indicated by several recent sources, the historiography of the westward movement is changing. Social historians are paying closer attention to ordinary people such as Alvin T. Smith. Further, studies on race, gender, class, and sexual behavior have refined scholars's views of the region and presented a much more complete picture of life on the frontier.[12] But in all of the fresh, new approaches to the West, few traditional historians have ventured into the realms of the built environment and material culture for sources.[13] Most historians are trained to interpret written evidence. Yet manuscripts record only a fraction of the past. Oral history, in some cases, documents recent history. But for the masses of illiterate craftsmen, slaves, laborers, and others for whom written records and oral history are absent, an interdisciplinary approach that includes interpreting material culture often provides the only vehicle for understanding their history.[14]

This inquiry will combine traditional research and material culture methodologies. Documentary evidence provides information about the early development of Greek Revival architecture and about Oregon's house owners and builders. America's architects and pattern book authors wrote books, letters, and articles and kept diaries to promote the Greek Revival style and record their aspirations for the nation's architectural maturity. Oregon's Greek Revival house builders and owners were literate as well. They discussed their strenuous trek across the plains and their efforts to better themselves on the frontier. They also revealed their roles in the California gold rush and the impact it had on their financial fortunes, allowing them to finally realize many of their hopes and dreams.

Yet the documentary sources these Oregonians left behind provide only fragmentary information about their houses and why they built them. The structures themselves communicate that the owners firmly established their roots in Oregon, that they were successful in their various business ventures, and that they maintained strong cultural ties with the East. These observations as well as the questions concerning the disbursement of structures and the motivations of owners in selecting Greek Revival architecture are answered using material culture methodologies.

The National Register of Historic Places and the Historic American Building Survey provide examples of several hundred recorded Greek Revival structures throughout the country.[15] Carpenter pattern books from the early 1800s illustrate the variety of plans and details available to builders. Material culture specialists have provided assistance in formulating basic questions for reading information about the builder from the structure, understanding the significance of the edifices at the time they were built, and placing buildings in the broader framework of the society in which they were constructed. Cultural geographers and folklorists have created the methodology and the substantial body of literature on the distribution of folk housing. Architectural historians have established a language for reading the styles and components of buildings and a methodology to interpret the time and place and form and function of structures in their individual and collective settings.[16]

The windfall of the California gold rush provided many Oregonians with enough wealth to build houses in any shape or style they chose. A handful chose the more modern Gothic Revival style, using Andrew Jackson Downing's *The Architecture of Country Houses* (1850) for guidance. A vast majority, however, built Greek Revival residences that were remarkably similar to the better houses of their former home states. Besides nostalgia and the symbol of status, they were attracted to the conservative, simple, neat symmetry these structures represented. The story of how Greek Revival architecture spread from coast to coast and why Oregonians selected this style is an important chapter in understanding the cultural maturity of the West and the nation.

2

The Genesis of a Style

Alvin T. Smith was born in Branford, Connecticut, in 1802. When he left New England some thirty years later, the architectural character there had changed from the colonial Federal and Adams styles to the recently adopted Greek Revival style. Greek Revival architecture did not magically appear in Branford in the late 1820s.[1] It developed in Europe in the mid-1700s with the excavation and pictorial recording of the ancient ruins of Italy and Greece. The fascination with these monuments had never really died; however, in this wave of interest, architects used the picture plates from recently published books to translate the antiquities into their designs in Europe and the United States. The revolution of modern Greece against the Ottoman Empire in the late 1700s and early 1800s provided yet another stimulus of interest in classical culture. Finally, American authors continued the European architectural publishing tradition by preparing pattern books that guided builders with pragmatic instructions for creating stylish houses. These factors contributed to the development, popularity, and spread of Greek Revival architecture.

THE REDISCOVERY OF ANCIENT GREECE AND ROME

During the mid-1700s, amateur archeologists tunneled into the long-buried Roman cities of Pompeii and Herculaneum and found the intact remains of villas, temples, markets, baths, and works of art. Soon, these newly discovered sites were included in the fashionable "grand tours" of European aristocrats and scholars. Goethe visited Pompeii in 1787. Johann Joachim Winkelmann visited the cities in the 1750s and 1760s, and his visits inspired his enormously influential work on modern art historical methodology, *Geschichte der Kunst des Altertums* (1764). His passion for the antiquities influenced the revival of classical art and architecture in Europe.[2] Edward Gibbon also explored the ancient Roman cities, then launched into writing his multivolume history classic, *Decline and Fall of the Roman Empire* (1776–1788).

Paralleling the discovery of Pompeii and Herculaneum, Europeans rediscovered the legacies of ancient Greece. Scholars faithfully reproduced the archeological remains of the antiquities for posterity in handsomely illustrated volumes. Englishmen James Stuart, a painter, and Nicolas Revett, an architect, were the first to envision an ambitious publication project. Their work went through several editions and was the most important of the recording efforts. Eventually, the Stuart and Revett work would include four volumes and would be called *The Antiquities of Athens* (1762 to 1818). In the preface to the first volume, Stuart clearly stated his opinion of Grecian culture when he wrote: "Greece was the great Mistress of the Arts, and Rome, in this respect, no more than her disciple; it may be presumed, all the most Admired Buildings which adorned that Imperial city, were but imitations of Grecian originals."[3]

The Stuart and Revett volumes were influential because they were well conceived and executed. They also became classic works of art. As the plate reproduced here (Figure 2.1) clearly shows, they prepared realistic drawings of their subjects. The Parthenon looks much as it did in the mid-1700s — a ruin surrounded by a variety of modern and medieval structures. Although published primarily for the enjoyment of the dilettantes of Europe, *The Antiquities of Athens* became one of the most significant architectural resources ever published. Designers in Europe and later in the United States incorporated features from these volumes into their work. Builders and architects no longer had to guess what the Parthenon looked like — they now had a published picture for guidance.

The buildings that resulted from this renaissance of interest were quite different from their ancient models. For one thing, Greek Revival architecture in Europe and the United States lasted for about a century, ranging from the high style structures designed by architects to the simple vernacular houses created by carpenters. Ancient Grecian architecture developed over six centuries. During that period, building design went through subtle refinements rather than fundamental changes. In fact, the Doric order remained virtually unchanged for several centuries.

When Iktinos was commissioned to design the Parthenon with an almost limitless budget, he brought together all of the centuries of Hellenic architectural refinement to create the most magnificent structure of his day. Perched on top of the acropolis, the site was ideal.

Figure 2.1: Drawing of the Parthenon, Athens, taken from Stuart James and Nicolas Revett, *The Antiquities of Athens*, 1762.

Then, he incorporated irregular features to relax the stiff appearance that would result from a perfect structure; he inclined the entablature outward to prevent it from seeming to lean inward; and he used a technique called entasis on the columns to give them a rounded, sprightly, and resilient appearance.[4]

The European and American designers in the eighteenth and nineteenth centuries did not have the centuries of architectural refinements in classical forms upon which to build. Instead they accommodated their Greek Revival designs to building forms and usages that had evolved over several millenia. For example, Hellenic temples quite literally housed Greek gods. European and American temples were called houses of God, but no physical dieties resided within. In short, the windows, interior spaces, and even the exterior architectural massing were different in their modern structures. Yet European architects designed archeologically correct classical orders and faithfully copied Greek monuments and temple facades as attachments or structural members into the modern houses of the elite and into new public buildings.[5]

AMERICAN HIGH STYLE GREEK REVIVAL ARCHITECTURE

Several European architects brought their Greek Revival experience and libraries to the United States. One of these individuals, Benjamin Henry Latrobe, made his grand tour of ancient antiquities in the late 1700s, traveling widely on the continent, observing the modern advancements in construction as well as the ancient buildings of Italy. He was particularly impressed with the design and acoustical qualities of the Pantheon in Rome and adapted its dome into many of his later American structures. When he returned to London, Latrobe learned civil engineering from John Smeaton and architecture from Samuel Pepys Cockerell. He developed a respectable practice there in private architecture and as an official surveyor for the London police.

In 1796 Latrobe decided to leave his homeland and seek fame and fortune in America. Soon after his arrival in Virginia, Latrobe began practicing his dual professions, and in the next twenty-four years, he introduced a new standard for design excellence with his buildings and engineering projects.[6] Within several months, Latrobe was hired to design the new Virginia State Penitentiary in Richmond. Soon, the Dismal Swamp Company, the James River Company, and the Upper Appomattox Navigation Company all requested his engineering expertise for their projects.

In 1798 he moved to Philadelphia to design the new Bank of Pennsylvania (Figure 2.2). The basic form was derived from the Greek Ionic temple on the Ilyssus near Athens, but the low central dome, broad wall surfaces, arched windows, central skylit vaulted banking hall, and simple finishing treatment throughout were his own innovations — inspired by his grand tour of the antiquities. His bank established a precedent for later American Greek Revival efforts. He was more interested in an eclectic approach to modern and ancient design than to authentically copying classical structures.[7] He articulated the differences in a letter to Thomas Jefferson:

> My principles of good taste are rigid in Grecian architecture. I am a bigoted Greek in the condemnation of the Roman architecture, . . . but the forms and distribution of Roman and Greek buildings which remain are in general inapplicable to the objects and uses of our public buildings. Our religion requires churches wholly different from the temples. . . . Our government, our legislative assemblies, and our courts of justice [are] buildings of entirely different principles from their basilicas.[8]

18

Figure 2.2: Bank of Pennsylvania, Philadelphia, Pennsylvania. Designed by Benjamin Latrobe, 1800. *Courtesy Independence National Historical Park.*

Shortly after his arrival in Philadelphia, Latrobe used his engineering skills to establish a new city water system. His scheme diverted water from the Schuylkill River into a reservoir, then distributed the water by gravity flow throughout the city. One phase of the project required a pumping station to lift the water into storage reservoirs. Latrobe designed a classical structure and skillfully masked the offices, boilers, and tank behind the cubical base with a Greek Doric columnated entrance and vaulted dome (Figure 2.3). Steam from the boilers rose through an opening in the dome, later prompting Latrobe's biographer to suggest that the building appeared as a Greco-Roman temple with smoke rising from the sacrificial altar.[9]

With his Bank of Pennsylvania and Philadelphia Water Works, Latrobe achieved a national reputation as an architect and engineer. He received commissions for the houses of such notables as Henry Clay and Stephen Decatur. He designed the Baltimore Cathedral, worked with Robert Fulton developing steamships for the Ohio River trade, and finished the design of a water system for New Orleans. His son had started the New Orleans water project, but had contracted yellow fever and died before the system was completed. Latrobe himself was struck by yellow fever and died in New Orleans in 1820. Before his death, however, he contributed to the development of this southern city by designing several elegant buildings in the French Quarter.[10]

Figure 2.3: Centre Square Pump Station, Philadelphia, Pennsylvania. Designed by Benjamin Latrobe, 1800. *Courtesy Independence National Historical Park.*

One of Latrobe's English contemporaries, George Hadfield, came to the United States at about the same time. Hadfield's credentials were impeccable. He graduated from the Royal Academy and won a gold medal for his outstanding academic performance. The academy rewarded him by sending him on a tour of Italy and then exhibiting his architectural renderings when he returned. He then apprenticed with some of England's finest architects and was well on his way to establishing a respectable career when he was offered the opportunity to supervise the construction of the new United States Capitol. Hadfield accepted the appointment and left England; but, shortly after his arrival, he discovered that the project was fraught with numerous political and technical problems. He left the capitol project before it was finished to design several other public buildings in the new capital. While working in Washington, Hadfield met George Washington Parke Custis, the adopted son of the first president, who commissioned him

Figure 2.4: Arlington House, Arlington, Virginia. Designed by George Hadfield, 1818. *Courtesy National Park Service.*

to design a mansion — Arlington House — on a site with a command-ing view of the capital city and the Potomac.

Custis hired Hadfield in 1803 or 1804, and construction began in 1808 and was completed in 1818 (Figure 2.4). The architect took full advantage of the site by designing a monumental Grecian temple form structure. The massive portico, supported by Doric columns that were twenty-three feet high by five feet wide at the base, could be seen from almost any point in the capital city. The design was decidedly Greek, to the exclusion of Roman or other classical details. Hadfield's temple-front format, with flanking wings became a model for pattern books and other Greek Revival houses from coast to coast. The Sam Brown house in Oregon would follow the same basic design pattern when the style reached the Pacific Northwest.[11]

In the European tradition, aspiring architects served apprentice-ships under master architects before they ventured out on their own. Along with his other talents, Latrobe was a gifted teacher as well. He took several young charges under his wings, encouraging them to accept challenging projects and instilling in them an appreciation for classical architectural forms. Of Latrobe's students, Robert Mills and William Strickland became the most prominent. Both achieved enviable reputations in their own rights. They designed some of the more noteworthy American buildings in the early 1800s, establishing many of the trends for Greek Revival architecture in the country.

Mills was born in Charleston, South Carolina, in 1781. He began his architectural career working for Irish architect James Hoban on the White House in Washington. In 1801 or 1802 he met Thomas Jefferson, who invited him to Charlottesville to study architecture and assist in the design and construction of Monticello. After Mills left Virginia, he traveled to several eastern cities on a "grand tour" of American building systems and then moved to Philadelphia at the suggestion of Jefferson to work in Latrobe's office.[12]

Mills worked for Latrobe for several years. Gradually he developed his own practice, accepting commissions to design churches in Philadelphia. For the Sansom Street Baptist Church, completed in 1809, Mills designed an auditorium with a seating capacity of four thousand. Mills accommodated the congregation within a octagonal-domed space, arranging the pews around a central platform and a huge baptismal, symbolizing the importance of this sacrament in the Baptist denomination. When completed, the local newspapers praised Mills's genius and stated that the acoustics were "the best to be found in the Union."[13]

Upon the completion of the Sansom Street church, Mills became a popular architect in Philadelphia. He designed residential and commerical structures and in 1811 planned and supervised the reconstruction of office wings on Independence Hall.[14] Next, he won a competition to design the Monumental Church in Richmond, Virginia, as a memorial to the victims of a major fire in that city. Mills borrowed the octagonal shape for the main structure from his Philadelphia Baptist church, then placed a ceremonial entrance on the front of the structure, similar in design to that of the Athenian treasury building in Delphi, with an urn at the center to represent the ashes of the fire's victims.[15]

In 1830 he was appointed principal draughtsman to the Land Office in Washington. He began preparing plans for marine hospitals, customs houses, federal buildings in Washington, and other public buildings around the country. Within three years, however, the Treasury Building, Post Office, and Patent Office burned, opening new opportunities for architects in the capital city. Following these fires, President Andrew Jackson appointed Mills to the position of architect

Figure 2.5: The Hermitage (Andrew Jackson House), Nashville, Tennessee. Unknown designer of portico, 1831. *Courtesy Tennessee State Library and Archives.*

and engineer for the federal government.[16] As evidence of his interest in the Greek Revival style of architecture, the president had recently remodeled the Hermitage (1831) by adding a large two-story front portico supported by ten slender Doric columns (Figure 2.5).[17] Jackson also was impressed with Mills's reputation for designing fireproof structures and thus promoted him to the position of chief architect for the capital in 1836.

Shortly after his appointment, Mills became the architect for the new Treasury Department Building. This structure would be much larger than his earlier efforts and far more complicated, since his superiors required a fireproof edifice. Mills subdivided the interior into vaulted masonry spaces. He provided convenient central corridors for access to and from the rooms and included primary and secondary stairways at strategic locations for safe exits. Realizing that the vaulted ceilings would place tremendous stress on the structural system, Mills used granite for the bearing walls.[18]

In addition to the impressive fireproofing system on the interior, Mills created a dramatic exterior appearance by placing a series of Ionic columns along the entire eastern exposure (336 feet) to conform with the monumental character of the existing Capitol and the White House (Figure 2.6). Several years following the completion of the structure, Greek style porticoes, which were specified in the original

Figure 2.6: United States Treasury Department Building, Washington, D.C. Designed by Robert Mills, 1842. *Courtesy National Park Service.*

plans, were added to the north and south facades to complete the classical design.[19]

Mills's final important work was the Washington Monument on the mall in Washington, which was completed after his death. In addition to his buildings, Mills also left a valuable written legacy for the practice of architecture. In a letter submitted with his proposal for a design contest, he stated why he selected the classical style for the project. Then he went on to suggest how the ancient forms should be viewed by his contemporaries:

> Greece it must be acknowledged brought the arts of design to a higher degree of perfection than any other nation, or at least established correct principles upon which to found them — so long as attention is paid to the rules laid down by them, we shall never offend the eye of genius and sophisticated taste.[20]

Mills was fond of Greek Revival architecture, but he also was a pragmatist and was not bound to using classical detailing on all of his

Figure 2.7: Second Bank of the United States, Philadelphia, Pennsylvania. Designed by William Strickland, 1824. *Courtesy Independence National Historical Park.*

designs. "Study your country's tastes and requirements," he wrote, "and make classic ground *here* for your art."[21]

Latrobe's other noteworthy student, William Strickland, came to the attention of his future teacher as the fourteen-year-old son of one of the carpenters on the Bank of Pennsylvania. Although he was quite young, Latrobe quickly recognized the young man's enormous talent, gave him responsible assignments, and, when Strickland left his employment, wrote him glowing recommendations.[22]

In 1818 Strickland finally received the opportunity to demonstrate his skill as an architect. He responded to a 12 May 1818 announcement in the *Pennsylvania Gazette* soliciting plans that would reflect "a chaste imitation of Grecian architecture, in its simplest and least expensive form" for the Second Bank of the United States.[23] Nicolas Biddle, a friend of several directors and later president of the bank, probably influenced the stipulation for a Greek design. Biddle had visited

Greece twelve years earlier on his grand tour and was a thorough-going philhellene in his architectural tastes. He and the board members probably anticipated a scheme similar to Latrobe's Bank of Pennsylvania. When the committee opened the proposals, however, it discovered that William Strickland's plan quite literally adopted the "Grecian" requirement (Figure 2.7).[24]

Strickland used a powerful Greek prototype for his model. "In the design and proportions of this edifice," he wrote in his proposal, "we recognize the leading features of that celebrated work of antiquity, the Parthenon in Athens." But he also recognized that "in selecting this example . . . it becomes a difficult task for an architect to preserve all the characteristics of a Grecian temple."[25] One problem was the interior space. A modern bank in the early 1800s required lighting, heating, and office spaces — features not considered in an ancient Greek temple. The architect tastefully incorporated these necessities into his plan and faithfully maintained the basic form and detailing of the Parthenon on the exterior. He selected the Greek Doric order for the porticoes on the front and rear facades, and enhanced these features with large marble columns and full pediments. Budgetary constraints and a restricted lot size forced him to delete the colonades from the sides and to design plain pediments instead of elaborately carved friezes typical of Athenian temples.

The Second Bank was an unusual form of Greek Revival architecture in that it sought to recreate a classical building in a modern setting. Americans were quite taken by the achievement of their fellow countryman; however, the most effusive praise came from foreign observers. August Levasseur, who published the Marquis de Lafayette's diary written during his return to the United States in 1824–25, said that "the new bank of the United States . . . is generally regarded as the finest specimen of architecture in the Union."[26] The *London Morning Chronicle* also praised the building in an 1837 article by saying, "[The Second Bank] excels in elegance and equals in utility, . . . not only the Bank of England, but . . . any banking house in the world."[27]

Strickland's bank impressed foreign and domestic observers, and it influenced American architecture almost from the moment the last marble panel was set in place. The charter that created the Second Bank enabled the institution to establish branch offices throughout the country. By 1831 twenty-four offices, from Portland, Maine, to New Orleans, Louisiana, controlled the nation's currency and fiscal policy. The directorate, which by then was under the leadership of Nicolas

Figure 2.8: Second Bank of the United States, Erie, Pennsylvania, branch, ca. 1828. *Courtesy Talbot Hamlin Collection, Avery Architecture Library, Columbia University.*

Biddle, recognized the value of classical office buildings and encouraged the branches to construct their new edifices in the Greek Revival style. The branch in Louisville, Kentucky, selected the temple of Bacchus in Teos as the prototype for its new building.[28] The Erie, Pennsylvania, branch constructed a simplified version of Strickland's bank with a Doric portico for its entrance (Figure 2.8).[29] Branches in Savannah, Georgia, Boston, Massachusetts, and Charleston, South Carolina, utilized classical detailing for their offices. The Wall Street branch in New York used an adaptation of classical detailing for its structure. The building has since been demolished, but the facade is incorporated into the entrance for the American Wing of the Metropolitan Museum of Art.

By the 1840s Greek Revival style banks were prevalent throughout the country. The National Bank of West Chester, Pennsylvania, hired Philadelphia architect — and Strickland's student — Thomas U. Walter to design a more delicate version of the Philadelphia Second Bank. The Bank of Indiana, with branches in all of the major towns and cities in the state, selected a standard classical porticoed front for its buildings.[30] It seemed that in many areas the classical design was to the

Figure 2.9: Merchants Exchange, Philadelphia, Pennsylvania. Designed by William Strickland, 1834. *Courtesy Independence National Historical Park.*

1800s banks what drive-in tellers are to the financial institutions of today.

Strickland's last major project in Philadelphia, the Merchants Exchange (1834), is an excellent expression of his skill as an architect (Figure 2.9). The triangular shape of the site posed an interesting design dilemma — that of locating a symmetrical classical structure on an asymmetrical lot. Strickland responded to the problem by placing a

Figure 2.10: Tennessee State Capitol, Nashville, Tennessee. Designed by William Strickland, 1858. *Courtesy Tennessee State Library and Archives.*

rounded Corinthian portico and tower — copied from the Choragic Monument of Lysicrates — at the narrow end of the triangle. Like the European architects in the Greek Revival style, Strickland incorporated an archeologically correct ancient monument into his modern design.

Strickland continued his Philadelphia practice until he accepted an invitation to design and build the new Tennessee State Capitol in 1844. When he arrived in Nashville, he discovered that the building site was on a hill, not unlike those used by ancient architects, and he set about devising a plan to take advantage of the setting. His scheme incorporated the Ionic order of the Erectheum for the end porticoes, topped with a dome based on the Choragic Monument of Lysicrates (Figure 2.10). Strickland's Tennessee capitol was his largest project, and in addition to the logistical problems with the structure itself, he had to contend with the state legislature. The officials did not provide enough funds to keep the project on schedule. Then, as construction lagged, they criticized Strickland for not moving fast enough. Strickland died

Figure 2.11: Founder's Hall, Girard College, Philadelphia, Pennsylvania. Designed by Thomas U. Walter, 1833. *Courtesy National Park Service.*

in 1854, three years before the completion of the capitol. His son Francis continued as supervisor of construction until the project was finished.[31]

Strickland, like his mentor, was a fine teacher. He probably thought of himself when he took Thomas U. Walter, the fifteen-year-old son of a bricklayer, into his office as an apprentice. Walter studied under Strickland for several years, then, when he felt he had learned enough to go into business for himself in 1829, he accepted several commissions in the Philadelphia area. In 1833 he was selected to design one of the most unusual and expensive projects of his day. Stephen Girard, a self-made, wealthy, and eccentric local businessman, stipulated in his will that a school for boys would be built on land he had set aside in Philadelphia. The budget would be virtually limitless, but the designer would be required to meet exacting specifications of design established by Girard (Figure 2.11).

As Walter was formulating plans for Girard College, he made a trip to Europe to study a number of buildings. He developed a plan that called for a Corinthian order structure, surrounded by a complete peristyle breezeway supported by thirty-four columns. On the interior, each floor was subdivided into four classrooms, accessed by magnificent stairways and Ionic-columned hallways. Walter managed to meet all of the design criteria established by Girard — especially

Figure 2.12: Andalusia (Nicolas Biddle Home), Philadelphia, Pennsylvania, 1798. Remodeled by Thomas U. Walter, 1835–36. *Courtesy National Park Service.*

the unlimited budget. Some estimates place the final price tag at $2,000,000. Nicolas Biddle was on the board that supervised the design and construction of Girard College. As Walter was working on the school, Biddle hired him to remodel his home on the banks of the Delaware River, north of Philadelphia. Walter added a large portico, with Doric columns and detailing based on the Theseum that could be seen from the Delaware. Biddle named his home Andalusia (Figure 2.12).[32]

John Haviland, another Englishman, also migrated to the United States to establish an architectural practice in Philadelphia. He designed St. Andrews Episcopal Church — now St. George's Greek Orthodox Church — and Franklin Institute — now the Atwater-Kent Museum — in the 1820s. He then turned to other design vocabularies, such as the Egyptian Revival, for his other work. Haviland was a fine architect; however, he made another equally important contribution to Greek Revival architecture by publishing the first American pattern book on the style. *The Builder's Assistant* (1818) provided American builders with clear, practical information and illustrations to guide them through the various steps of designing and building Greek Revival edifices.[33]

A number of other fine architects contributed their creativity to the development of the Greek Revival style as well. Their work is adequately covered in other sources. The designers discussed here were among the earliest and most influential. Latrobe, Hadfield, and Haviland brought their considerable experience in European Greek Revival architecture — as well as their copies of pattern books — to the United States. They, in turn, translated their ideas into the American setting and trained American students to carry on their tradition.

SYMBOLS OF DEMOCRACY

One building in particular, one building in which four of these architects played some role, became a national symbol that was copied in nearly every state in the union. The National Capitol, with its central dome and flanking wings, became this model. Architectural historians debate as to whether the capitol's principal style is Greek Revival; they agree, however, that many of its major characteristics and details are Greek Revival.

The new capitol building was completed after many long and trying years. Congress had authorized the new building in 1792, while the capital was located in Philadelphia, and instructed President George Washington to appoint a commission to solicit plans. The committee selected the design submitted by Dr. William Thornton, and it hired another architect, Stephen Hallet, to supervise construction. None of the principals — the legislative and executive branches and the architects — had any concept of the magnitude of this project. Thus, the finished capitol required nearly forty years and six architects, not to mention a fire during the War of 1812, before the first phase was completed in 1835.[34]

This phase included the vision of Dr. Thornton, who first had conceived the plan, and Charles Bulfinch, who made some of the final changes and saw the project through to completion. George Hadfield contributed his expertise and Robert Mills designed the floor of the House of Representatives chamber (now Statuary Hall). The monumental character throughout and the unique Greek Revival detailing on the interior were the results of Benjamin Latrobe's influence.

Latrobe was hired by President Thomas Jefferson in 1802 as the surveyor of public buildings of the United States.[35] One of the major duties of this position was the completion of the National Capitol. Shortly after Latrobe arrived in Washington, he noted major flaws in Thornton's structural system and began revising the plans and correcting the apparent problems, such as leaking roofs and cracked plaster.[36] Latrobe was openly critical of Thornton's plan, calling it a "poverty of design," which attracted the ire of the doctor's friends in Congress. The congressmen who were not his friends were concerned

Figure 2.13: National Capitol, Washington, D.C. Designed by Benjamin Latrobe et al., 1835. *Courtesy Avery Library.*

about Latrobe's propensity for consistently overspending his appropriated budget. Jefferson, however, was willing to fight Latrobe's political battles, because he saw the capitol as the "first temple dedicated to the sovereignty of the people, embellishing with Athenian taste the cause of a nation looking far beyond the range of Athenian destinies."[37]

Latrobe was conscious that the capitol was enormously important to the city of Washington and the young republic. He based most of his ideas on classical examples, but he modified some of the ancient motifs with American symbols. For instance, he incorporated stocks of Indian maize into the columns and capitals in the entryway to the House and the Supreme Court, which became the most popular features among the members of Congress. To execute these and other artistic components, Latrobe and Jefferson convinced Congress to appropriate sufficient funds to bring two talented stonemasons from Italy.[38] In the Senate rotunda, Latrobe created delicate tobacco-leaf capitals for the Corinthian columns in the place of traditional Greek acanthus leaves. Latrobe's capitol became a national shrine for all Americans (Figures 2.13–2.15). The classical detailing and the rotunda-dome-wing plan to which Latrobe, Thornton, and Bulfinch contributed became a model for statehouses from New England to Oregon.

In addition to serving as an architectural prototype, the National Capitol provided another more practical benefit. Committees in charge of public building projects recognized that professional designers could deliver plans for attractive structures and, in some cases,

Figure 2.14: Cornstalk capital, National Capitol, Old House Rotunda, 1835. *Photo Robert K. Sutton.*

Figure 2.15: Tobacco-leaf capitals, National Capitol, Old Senate Rotunda, 1835. *Photo Robert K. Sutton.*

save them money. This revelation required the expert salesmanship of designers such as Ithiel Town. Town and his partner, Alexander Jackson Davis, established one of the earliest and most successful American architectural firms on the basis of their state capitol contracts. In 1827 Town presented a proposal to the Connecticut Statehouse Committee for a new capitol that specified an inexpensive Greek Doric temple with a minimum of detailing. Town's plan was accepted, and when the project was underway, Alexander Davis became a partner. The arrangement was beneficial to both men. Town, bored with design and building details, preferred traveling around the country promoting his bridge truss and architectural firm. Davis, on the other hand, enjoyed drawing sketches, preparing plans, and overseeing the projects from the firm's New York City office.[39]

Upon completion of the Connecticut Statehouse, Town's salesmanship secured a contract in 1832 to design the new Indiana State Capitol in Indianapolis (Figure 2.16). In characteristic fashion, Davis drew the plans and Town handled the negotiations with the building committee and contractors.[40] The design combined a representation of the Parthenon with a ribbed Renaissance Revival dome.[41] Soon after

Figure 2.16: Indiana Statehouse, Indianapolis, Indiana. Designed by Town and Davis, 1832. *Courtesy Avery Library.*

the Indiana project was underway, Town secured another contract to design a statehouse for North Carolina. Here Davis corrected the problem of mixing styles by developing a classical building with a central rotunda. A Greek portico entrance was flanked with wings, and the structure was topped with an unobtrusive dome.[42]

While the Indiana Statehouse project was underway, Vermont voted to build a new capitol. In 1831 it appointed a building committee to secure plans for a statehouse. Committee members traveled to New Hampshire, Massachusetts, and Connecticut to study the neighboring capitols, and then hired Ammi B. Young, from Burlington, as its architect. Working with the committee, Young devised a plan that incorporated the configuration and dome of the Massachusetts Statehouse and the Greek Doric detailing of Town's Connecticut Capitol. In 1833 the committee members reported that their architect had "prepared a plan for a building which they flatter themselves, will be found in point of convenience, second to no one in the United States and which, in its external appearance and architectural proportions, will be creditable to the State."[43]

Young's design was based on a plan of the Greek Doric Temple of Theseus and published in Edward Shaw's *Civil Architecture* (1832). The principal features included a copper-sheathed wooden saucer dome and a formal front portico (Figure 2.17). Granite was the primary

Figure 2.17: Vermont Statehouse, Montpelier, Vermont. Designed by Ammi B. Young, 1836. *Courtesy First Vermont Bank and Trust Company.*

building material.[44] Vermonters were proud of their capitol, and the building drew the attention of *The American Magazine of Useful Knowledge*. In an 1836 issue, the periodical stated that it was "beautiful alike in design, architectural character and execution. . . . [Its] design is very neat and simple, a chaste architectural character preserved throughout the whole."[45]

Following the completion of the Vermont Statehouse, Young went to Boston and planned the United States Customs House. In 1852 he replaced Robert Mills as the supervising architect of the Treasury Department and designed governmental buildings from coast to coast.[46] Young was working in Washington when his Vermont capitol was damaged by fire in 1858. A new architect, J. R. Richards of Boston, was placed in charge of the rehabilitation. He added a more prominent dome, but in deference to Young's plan, he maintained the original Greek format on the main body.[47]

During the 1830s and 1840s, several states and territories built new capitols. In 1833 Arkansas hired George Weigart from Lexington, Kentucky, to prepare plans for a Territorial Assembly Building in Little Rock. Weigart created a Greek Doric Temple plan similar to Town's

Figure 2.18: Arkansas State Capitol, Little Rock, Arkansas. Designed by George Weigart, 1836. *Courtesy Stephen L. Recken.*

Figure 2.19: Missouri Statehouse, Jefferson City, Missouri. Designed by Stephen Hills, ca. 1848. *Courtesy Avery Library.*

Connecticut Statehouse. He placed the structure on a hill overlooking the Arkansas River, and thus presented a visual effect similar to Strickland's Tennessee Capitol (Figure 2.18).[48] Missouri commissioned Stephen Hills from Pennsylvania to design and supervise the construction of a statehouse in Jefferson City (Figure 2.19).[49] The Territory of Florida built a capitol in Tallahassee, and the legislature's foresighted planning was, in part, responsible for transforming the capital city from a "shanty town" into a modern community.[50]

Other states and territories constructed capitols between 1830 and 1860. Generally building committees and architects worked together to create statehouses that would emulate, as closely as possible, the finest architecture in the country. In towns such as Tallahassee, the new state capitol was the catalyst for establishing a modern capital as well. Several common ingredients were shared by these statehouses. Most were classical in style, and many adopted the rotunda-dome-wing design formula. Greek Revival capitols were so popular and pervasive, they appeared even in the Far West — in California and Oregon.

California became a state as the result of the Compromise of 1850, which, for ten years, assuaged northern and southern interests. The gold rush brought an influx of thousands of new residents, and California achieved statehood without the customary territorial waiting period. During the first two years of statehood, the California legislature met in temporary headquarters; then, in 1853, the community of Benicia invited the government to use its new Greek Revival building as the capitol. The legislature accepted the offer and housed the government there for a year.

A local tradition suggests that the carpenter in charge based his design on a painting of Thomas Jefferson's Virginia State Capitol. Perhaps the artwork was poor, or more likely such a painting did not exist, for the Benicia capitol bore little resemblance to the Richmond statehouse. Some of the features were similar, such as the general configuration and the placement of modillions within the pediment, but as a whole, the Benicia capitol was a vernacular combination of classical details (Figure 2.20). Another, more plausible, tradition states that some of the lumber and the interior columns were salvaged from ships abandoned in San Francisco harbor during the early stages of the gold rush.[51]

Unlike her neighbor to the south, Oregon was first a territory in 1848 before becoming a state in 1859. Oregon's path to statehood, however, was not entirely conventional. In 1843, before the Pacific

Figure 2.20: California Statehouse, Benicia, California. Unknown designer, 1851. *Courtesy Avery Library.*

Northwest was officially divided between the United States and Great Britain, settlers met at Champoeg in the Willamette Valley to establish a provisional government. The system was rudimentary, with a judge, a legislative committee, and an executive committee of three representing the three branches of government. Iowa's first territorial session of 1838 and the federal Northwest Ordinance of 1787 served as bases for the code of laws. The provisional system granted settlers 640 acres of land, established a militia of three rifle companies, and divided the land area into counties. There were no taxes, which, in retrospect, probably made the government palatable to the populace. Provisional authorities claimed jurisdiction over the area between California and Alaska.[52]

For nearly eleven years, Oregon's provisional and territorial governments met in the open air, churches, private residences, and commercial buildings in Oregon City and Salem. In 1849, a year after Oregon became a territory, Congress appropriated $25,000 for a capitol building.[53] Before the money could be spent, however, the legislature first needed to decide on a location for the capital city. In 1851 it voted

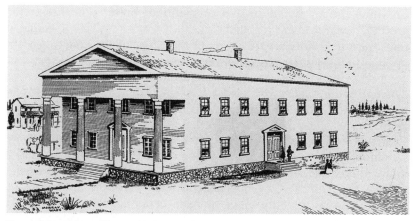

Figure 2.21: Oregon Territorial Capitol, Salem, Oregon. Unknown designer, 1855. *Courtesy Oregon Historical Society.*

to move from Oregon City to Salem. Once the legislators made this decision, they appointed a building committee and selected a site. By 1853 the committee had secured a set of plans (prepared by an unknown designer, and had hired Charles Bennett, a local builder, to construct the foundation for $8,913.[54]

Although the orginal plans no longer exist, the territorial records indicate that the design specified a stone structure, featuring a portico, Ionic columns, and classical detailing throughout. The sixth territorial legislature met in the partially completed structure in 1854, and during the session, the members realized that the appropriated funds would not be sufficient to finish the capitol. At that point, the legislature ordered the building committee to change the materials from stone to wood and simplify the detailing from Ionic to Doric (Figure 2.21).[55] The committee made the modifications and assured the legislature that the project would remain within the allocated budget.

Before the structure was completed, however, J. C. Avery from Benton County introduced a measure to move the seat of government to Corvallis. The legislature adopted the proposal, and on 3 December 1855, it moved the thirty-four miles to its new headquarters. These lawmakers were fickle, though, and five days later, they voted to return to Salem. Perhaps the legislators knew they would return to Salem, or perhaps a local businessman took an interest in the structure, because the capitol was finished and ready for the government's return on 17 December. Five days later the legislature adjourned for the

Christmas holidays, and on 29 December, the building burned to the ground.[56] Many Salem residents and the local newspaper speculated that a group from Corvallis had set the fire, but the committee appointed to investigate could not prove arson.[57]

Following the fire, the legislature decided to remain in Salem, and eventually the state constructed a statehouse similar to Latrobe's National Capitol. The new structure was larger and more decorative, but its history was less intriguing than that of its predecessor. A surviving sketch of the first capitol shows that it was an unusually plain representation of Greek Revival architecture. Four fluted Doric colums, a plain entablature, and an undecorated pediment comprised the front portico. On the rest of the exterior, pediments over the front and side doorways were the only other classical detailing. Still the structure anticipated the Greek Revival houses of Oregon's Willamette Valley.

The statehouse building committee had decided to erect a Greek Ionic stone building, reminiscent of Town's Connecticut Statehouse in form and Strickland's Tennessee Capitol in style. The surviving records, however, do not indicate the factors that influenced its choice. Clearly the committee wanted a functional, relatively inexpensive structure that would survive the wet Oregon winters.[58] No one complained when, as an economic measure, the committee members simplified the detailing and substituted wood for stone as the building material.

Not long after the Oregon capitol burned, Congress hired Thomas U. Walter to remodel and enlarge the National Capitol. He added new House and Senate chambers and designed a new dome supported with cast iron ribbing. Ironically, this building, which had served as a national architectural and governmental symbol, was remodeled to resemble the statehouses that had evolved from its original design.

THE GREEK REVOLUTION

In his annual presidential message of 1822, James Monroe recognized an important event in Europe — the Greek Revolution for independence from Turkey — and voiced the sentiments of many Americans, saying:

> The mention of Greece fills the mind with the most exalted sentiments and arouses in our bosoms the best feeling of which our nature is susceptible. Superior skill and refinement in arts, heroic gallantry in action, disinterested patriotism, enthusiastic zeal and devotion in

42

favor of public and personal liberty are associated with our recollections of Greece. . . . A strong hope is entertained that these people will
recover their independence and resume their equal station among
the nations of the earth.[59]

Only a year later, references to the Greek cause were conspicu-
ously absent from the president's report to Congress, as the administration officially declared neutrality in European affairs through the
Monroe Doctrine. Although the national government disclaimed interest in such political struggles across the sea, many private citizens
expressed their support for the revolutionaries by venturing to the
war zone to fight alongside the Greeks or by financial contributions to
the cause. Also, there was a renewed interest in ancient Greek culture.
Towns adopted names such as Syracuse, Utica, and Ithaca. College
fraternal organizations became the campus "greeks" and used letters
from the Greek alphabet for their names. Some Americans wore what
they perceived to be Athenian clothing, and others formed learned
societies called athenaeums. As a more lasting result, classical structures became patterns for new houses and buildings.

Interest in the Greek Revolution was short-lived, and within ten
years, most people had forgotten the cause. For a brief time, however,
the rebellion stirred the imagination of many Americans. Further, in
Boston and the Northeast, the development of Greek Revival architecture coincided closely with support for the revolt and acted as a
catalyst for the spread of the style.

To most Americans, this interest in the Greek Revolution is a
long-forgotten footnote in their history. At that time, however, the
revolt was the cause célèbre among the nation's intellectuals. Periodi-
cals carried accounts of Turkish atrocities against the Greeks and
stirred public support by equating this independence movement with
the American Revolution. Edward Everett, a respected professor of
classical literature at Harvard, became a champion of the revolutionaries and used his influence to make Boston a center for American
philhellenism. As editor of the *North American Review*, Everett reported
on the events in Greece and solicited support for the revolt.[60] In the
October 1823 issue, he reviewed A. Koreas's recent edited version of
the *Ethics of Aristotle* (1821) and concluded with an empassioned plea
for Americans to support the Greeks. Later that year Everett published
the text of a petition from the Messenian Senate at Calamata that read:
"the fellow citizens of Penn, of Washington, and of Franklin, will not
refuse their aid to the descendants of Phoecian, and Thrasybulus, of

Aratus, and of Philopoeman." At the end of the entreaty, Everett asked Boston to donate $10,000 and for New York, Philadelphia, Baltimore, and the cities of the South to raise money according to their means. Young men were invited to fight the Turks, "as the same class of generous spirits did . . . [for] this country in the revolutionary war."[61]

Support for the revolt took many forms. Throughout the country, committees were formed to raise money, and the New York group alone donated over $35,000.[62] Student organizations at Yale, Columbia, West Point, and other colleges contributed their time and money. Political leaders such as Daniel Webster and Governor William Eustis of Massachusetts were active supporters of the movement. In the spring of 1824, some of the more ardent young philhellenists actually went to Europe to fight with the Greek army. Jonathan P. Miller, a veteran of the War of 1812, volunteered for the cause, and the Boston committee subsidized his travel and equipment expenses.[63]

At the same time Boston was at the forefront of the political movement, it was also experiencing a more subtle architectural transformation. During the early nineteenth century, Boston had remained conservative in its tastes. Charles Bulfinch designed the Massachusetts Capitol, the Tontine Crescent (a semicircular row of houses), and other structures in the Federal style. In 1817 Bulfinch left Boston to become the architect for the National Capitol. Not long after his departure, new buildings gradually became more Greek in appearance. Alexander Parris, one of Bulfinch's associates, designed St. Paul's Church in 1819 with an entrance portico and a simple Ionic pediment.[64]

After 1820 Greek Revival architecture blossomed in Boston. Robert Mills showed an understanding of the cultural climate when he submitted a design for the Bunker Hill Monument. In his explanatory letter of 1825, he stated that ancient architects influenced all of his building ideas.[65] The committee did not select Mills's plan, rather chosing a scheme by Soloman Willard that was even more "Greek," with a stylized Doric temple pavilion adjacent to the monumental obelisk (Figures 2.22–2.23).[66] Alexander Parris's later designs also reflected a change in taste. His Quincy Market, erected in 1825 next to Faneuil Hall, copied the concepts of Latrobe's Bank of Pennsylvania — with a low central dome and end porticoes — and made a complete break with Boston's colonial tradition (Figure 2.24).

For more than a decade, major new construction in Boston demonstrated an interest in Greek culture. The Tremont House (1829), designed by Isaiah Rogers, was an early hotel in America (Figure 2.25). It featured many single and family rooms, a bank of reception rooms

Figure 2.22: Bunker Hill Monument, Boston, Massachusetts. Designed by Soloman Willard, 1825. *Courtesy of Richard B. Tourangeau.*

Figure 2.23: Bunker Hill Monument Pavilion, Boston, Massachusetts. Designed by Soloman Willard, 1825. *Courtesy of Richard B. Tourangeau.*

Figure 2.24: Quincy Market, Boston, Massachusetts. Designed by Alexander Parris, 1825. *Courtesy Avery Library.*

Figure 2.25: Tremont House, Boston, Massachusetts. Designed by Isaiah Rogers, 1829. *Courtesy Avery Library.*

and parlors opening from the rotunda, and a magnificent dining room.[67] William Havard Eliot published a richly illustrated book to celebrate the grand opening of the structure. He was careful to mention that the ceilings over the entrance and in the dining room were copied from the Propylaea at Eleusis. The stained glass in the circular skylight of the rotunda, Eliot noted, was influenced by the Baths of Titus in Rome. Further, the columns in the drawing room were patterned after the Temple of Minerva Polias.[68]

Ammi B. Young's Boston Customs House continued in the Greek tradition; but even before this building was completed, the city was beginning to adopt the newer Gothic Revival style.[69] Several prominent Bostonians grew tired of classical designs and suggested that the transplantation of antiquities into a modern setting was inappropriate. One such brahmin, Arthur Gilman, used a review of Edward Shaw's recent edition of *Rural Architecture* (1843) as a vehicle to criticize Greek Revival buildings in Boston. He began by referring to the Young's Customs House as something "so incongruous and absurd a pile, that we scarcely know where to begin or where to end our enumeration of its deformities." Gilman berated other classical structures and concluded by advocating an eclectic approach to architecture based on the Gothic style, which borrowed from the colonial and English traditions. "In these," he wrote, "we rejoice to perceive an increased knowledge and a growing taste."[70]

While Bostonians embraced the newer Gothic style, Greek Revival architecture spread into other New England towns. In some cases, Boston architects directly influenced building tastes in other areas. Alexander Parris and Isaiah Rogers designed houses and commercial buildings in Maine.[71] Cities and villages generally adopted Greek Revival architecture concurrently with the region's economic prosperity during the early 1800s. Merchants and sea captains built opulent mansions in coastal towns. Manufacturers constructed Greek Revival houses, places of business, and cottages for their workers in the rapidly developing industrial centers. Lumbermen chose the Greek Revival style for their residences near the northeastern timberland.

Many New England port communities became showcases for classical architecture in the early 1800s. Nantucket prospered as a whaling center, then lost a large segment of its population and its economic base when kerosene and gas replaced whale oil in in the mid-1800s. The business disaster, however, became a benefit for historic preservation and twentieth-century tourism, since its building stock remained virtually intact.[72] Some classical houses are testaments to the extravagance of the very rich, with heavy fluted columns supporting pedimented porticoes, large pilasters on the corners, and full entablatures surrounding the eaves. A majority of the middle-class residences were more restrained in their classical detailing. Few of these dwellings included porticoes, but in the place of a formal porch, the Doric or Ionic motifs were integrated into the molding surrounding the doorway. Capped pilasters supported full entablatures and entrances were recessed to provide shelter from the elements and to simulate temple fronts. Where molding replaced the portico, usually the same classical order was carried to and enlarged on the corner support pilasters and the entablatures.[73]

For some New England communities, such as Bangor, Maine, classical architecture was its first exposure to a formal style. During the early nineteenth century, the woodsmen exploited the plentiful northern forests to provide lumber for the Northeast.[74] The timber barons invested their profits in beautiful Greek Revival houses along Broadway Street in Bangor (Figures 2.26–2.27).[75]

Figure 2.26: Streetscape of Broadway Street Historic District, Bangor, Maine. Various builders, 1830s. *Courtesy The Maine Historic Preservation Commission.*

PUBLISHED SOURCES FOR GREEK REVIVAL ARCHITECTURE

In addition to fine mansions in Bangor and elsewhere, Maine also has an impressive collection of vernacular Greek Revival houses. Joyce Bibber discusses these structures in a recent book on the subject. Residents were so taken by the style, many remodeled their existing houses by adding classical architrave moldings, columns, and pilasters. Bibber also notes that new construction technology — such as planing, milling, and glassmaking — made stylish houses available to the middle class. Carpenters designed and built these houses, using other houses and architectural pattern books for guidance.

An earlier publication — The Historic American Building Survey catalogue for Maine (1974) — discusses these builder's handbooks as well. The authors mention that one or more portions of six Greek Revival residences in different parts of the state were derived from illustrative plates in the nineteenth-century pattern books of Asher Benjamin.[76] In New England and elsewhere, books by Benjamin and others provided the requisite information to educate carpenters on the techniques necessary to build classical structures.

Figure 2.27: Greek Revival house, Broadway Street Historic District, Bangor, Maine. Various builders, 1830s. *Courtesy The Maine Historic Preservation Commission.*

Architectural historians, cultural geographers, and folklorists have long known about and recognized the importance of pattern books. Until Dell Upton tackled the subject in a major article in 1984, however, few scholars had attempted to analyze these sources in a comprehensive fashion. Upton found that between 1797 and 1860, 188 architectural handbooks were published by American presses. He also discovered that the number of books printed increased almost geometrically toward the end of that period. Before 1800 there were two books available, but between 1850 and 1860, builders could choose from ninety-three new sources. With each new edition or volume, authors provided more sophisticated information to their readers, encouraging more competence and independence. Benjamin and his contemporaries also influenced architectural tastes. They modified classical orders, recognizing — or perhaps encouraging — practicality and simplicity.

Upton found that the authors of pattern books substantially influenced the development of vernacular architecture. They were successful because they built upon knowledge builders already possessed. Carpenters were familiar with floor plans and building types; they were, however, anxious to acquire the skills necessary to make their structures fashionable. Thus, to build a Greek Revival house, the builder would concentrate on the information necessary to create the Ionic or Doric order, then incorporate those features into the familiar plan, such as the I-house. By adding capitals to the structural corner pilasters and by attaching molding to the cornice boards, the basic Greek Revival house took form. With a little extra effort, the columns supporting the front porch could be topped with capitals, creating a simple portico. Then, several years later, when the taste of the customer changed again, the same builder could adapt to yet another style — such as Gothic Revival — by attaching vertical board-and-batten siding, adding pointed arches to dormer windows, and attaching gingerbread trim to the same basic structure (Figure 2.28).[77]

The American pattern book authors borrowed ideas from European counterparts and from each other. They adapted their material to keep current with popular styles. Their impact on American architecture, however, was quite different from that of Stuart and Revett on European architecture. The Englishmen published realistic plates of the antiquities primarily for the enjoyment of their readers. The designers who used these volumes as patterns, adapted actual antique structures into their work. On the other hand, American authors presented bits and pieces of ancient architecture — such as the composition of

Figure 2.28: Gothic Revival details. Taken from Andrew Jackson Downing *The Architecture of Country Houses*, 1850.

Ionic columns — to their customers. The buildings they illustrated were not Greek temples; they were drawings of generic American Greek Revival houses. Thus, the lack of concern for authenticity that started with Latrobe and his students became even more pronounced in the vernacular phase of the style.

Of the pattern book authors, Benjamin was the earliest and the most influential for domestic Greek Revival architecture. He was born in Hartford, Connecticut, in about 1773 and was trained by a local carpenter. Then he worked in the Connecticut River Valley for about fifteen years. In 1803 he moved to Boston where he worked for Charles Bulfinch.[78] Benjamin was a skilled craftsman, but if his structures had remained the only criteria for judgment, his role in American building history would have been minimal. His major contributions were the seven carpenter's handbooks he published between 1797 and 1843. Although the three earliest volumes, which appeared from 1797 to 1814, were based in part on the works of the English architects James Gibbs and Sir William Chambers, Benjamin adapted this material to his American audience.[79] Through the nearly fifty years Benjamin published his pattern books, he continuously revised his material to make it relevant to the needs of his readers.

When it became clear that Americans had adopted the Greek Revival style, he incorporated into his books the classical orders, detailing, and techniques necessary for carpenters to erect these structures. For example, the sixth edition of his *American Builder's Companion* (1827) included a notice by the publisher announcing that "Grecian Doric and Ionic architecture from the most celebrated remains of antiquity" was added to the previous edition to provide excellent classical examples for the readers (Figures 2.29–2.30).[80] The major difference between this and earlier editions was the illustrated Greek Revival detailing. Builders could build virtually the same house using either edition; with the sixth, however, they could add the now fashionable Greek motifs. Benjamin's later books expanded the instructions for exterior and interior classical features, offering more architectural variety.[81]

Benjamin's guidance was evident in many structures throughout the country. His books, however, did not include complete building plans. Thus, identifying his influences requires detective work to locate features such as fireplace mantles, moldings, or doorways. For instance, one architectural historian has analyzed Benjamin's contributions in Ohio and concluded that craftsmen there relied heavily on his pattern books. The most convincing example was the discovery of

Figure 2.29: Geometric detail for Ionic capital. Taken from Asher Benjamin, *American Builder's Companion*, 1827.

Figure 2.30: Detail for Ionic capital. Taken from Asher Benjamin *American Builder's Companion*, 1827.

Figure 2.31: Burritt Blakeslee House, Medina, Ohio. Unknown builder, ca. 1835. *Courtesy National Park Service.*

Figure 2.32: Sunbury Tavern, Sunbury, Ohio. Unknown builder, ca. 1820. *Courtesy National Park Service.*

a copy of Benjamin's *Practical House Carpenter* (1830) in the attic of the Burritt Blakeslee house near Medina a hundred years after it was built (Figure 2.31).[82] Eave cornices on the Sunbury Tavern in Sunbury (Figure 2.32) were patterned after a plan in the same book, and the pediment for an old bank in Marietta was derived from a plate in the *American Builder's Companion* (1827). Detailing features for other buildings in Ohio were similar to drawings in Benjamin's books.[83]

When Greek Revival architecture reached the West Coast, carpenters were both the designers and builders of most structures. Although no one to date has discovered copies of Benjamin's books in the attics of Oregon houses, similarities between particular details and illustrations in his books suggest that some carpenters had access to his works. For instance, a fireplace mantle in the Chatham Hawley House in Monroe, Oregon (1855), incorporated a Greek fret design nearly identical to a plate in Benjamin's *The Builder's Guide* (1837) (Figures 2.33–2.34).[84] Clearly, at least one Oregon builder carried a copy of Benjamin across the plains. The evidence, however, suggests that he was rare among Oregon carpenters. Pioneer museum collections around the state hold a rich assortment of the tools used to make Greek Revival details. Yet there are no copies of pattern books in the book collections donated by pioneer families. Further, a cursory analysis of the inventories of property in probate records indicate that Oregon builders did not have these sources in their libraries when they died.[85]

Although this study has not uncovered copies of pattern books, evidence presented by the buildings themselves suggests that Oregon builders were, nonetheless, familiar with the information these sources imparted. Many details on houses in Oregon likely were designed either by builders who had constructed Greek Revival houses elsewhere or by craftsmen who had observed classical details on buildings, then acquired the necessary tools to fashion these features. For example, the carpenter who crafted the front veranda on the Wolf Creek Tavern in Oregon may not have read a pattern book; yet he perhaps observed this detail on a structure such as the Sunbury Tavern. He carried the image in his mind, then translated his impression of the design into the Oregon tavern (Figure 2.35).

Asher Benjamin's works were not the only volumes available to carpenters in the early 1800s.[86] Among the authors who published books on Greek Revival architecture, one of the most gifted was Minard Lafever. Lafever received his training as a carpenter in upstate New York, then moved to New York City in 1828 where he spent

Figure 2.33: Greek fret detail on fireplace mantle of Jacob Spores House (formerly in Chatham Hawley House), Coburg, Oregon, 1855. *Courtesy Gregg Olsen.*

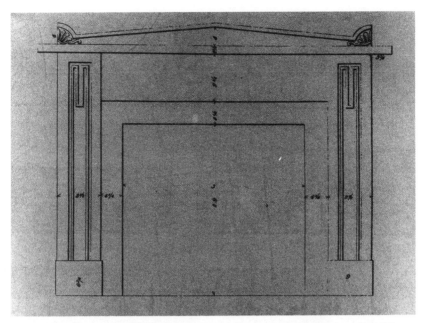

Figure 2.34: Greek fret design. Taken from Asher Benjamin, *The Builder's Guide*, 1837.

Figure 2.35: Wolf Creek Tavern, Wolf Creek, Oregon. Unknown designer, ca. 1878. *Courtesy Oregon State Parks.*

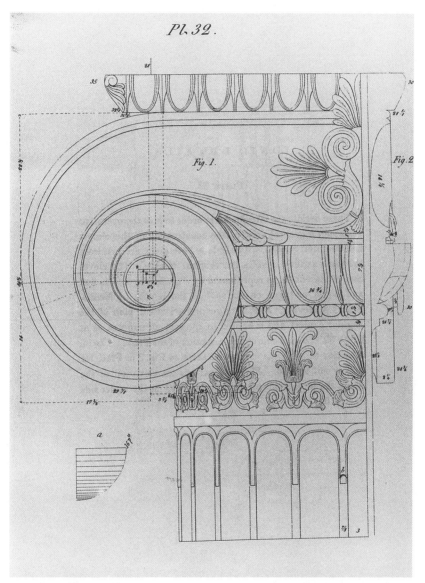

Figure 2.36: Ionic column detail. Taken from Minard Lafever, *The Beauties of Modern Architecture*, 1835.

several years as a builder and draftsman. He studied architecture in his spare time. His first publishing effort, *The Young Builder's General Instructor* (1829), presented general principles of carpentry and basic architecture. Lafever, though, was a perfectionist; he grew dissatisfied with the book and withdrew it from circulation within four years.[87] A year later, he wrote his next book, *The Modern Builder's Guide*, which became an instant success. He wrote this work in association with James Gallier and James H. Dakin, men who later became successful designers in their own rights. The combined effort was remarkably artistic and sophisticated. In his preface, Lafever acknowledged the influence of the English designers Peter Nickolson, James Stuart, and Nicolas Revett, but he also noted the advice of a local builder from Philadelphia, Joshua Coulter.[88]

The title of Lafever's third book, *The Beauties of Modern Architecture* (1835), revealed the elegance of Greek Revival architecture in America. By the mid-1830s the classical style was popular, and Lafever devoted most of his book to illustrating the design mode. Lafever's instructions and plates demonstrated how to construct an entire classical house. He provided plans, diagrams for executing details, and lithographic prints showing the finished product (Figure 2.36). His books encouraged craftsmen to use restraint and to strive for delicacy in their designs.[89] Thus Lafever's works provided excellent guidance to his readers and gave them the opportunity to incorporate exquisite detailing into their work.[90]

A number of other architectural sources became available during the early 1800s. In New England, Edward Shaw's *Rural Architecture* rivaled Benjamin's books in popularity. Between 1831 and 1876 Shaw's volume was printed in eleven editions and revised to reflect current styles and tastes. Although the content was similar to Benjamin's works, the format offered a more complete builder's handbook, with an emphasis on geometry and construction techniques.[91]

A recently published book, *Families and Farmhouses in 19th Century America* by Sally McMurry (1988), addresses yet another source of building plans and diagrams available to builders. From 1830 progressive farmers subscribed to a variety of agricultural journals to find out about new, promising experiments with crops, farm animals, and fertilizers. They discussed such topics as machinery, farm organizations, and agricultural education as well. McMurry focused on the informal exchange of farmhouse plans, which became an important component of these journals between 1830 and 1900. During that period, she discovered that several hundred such plans were published in eleven northern journals. Although McMurry primarily is interested in changes in residential spatial relationships, examples of the plans she includes reveal that farmers were interested in the appearance of their houses as well. Several agriculturalists used this forum to show off their new Greek Revival houses. Perhaps progressive Oregon farmers read these agricultural journals as they planned the designs of their Greek Revival houses.[92]

The rediscovery of ancient Greece and Rome stimulated a new interest in the architecture of these civilizations. Architects in Europe and the United States copied features from the monuments and temples of antiquity into their modern buildings. Americans adopted classical details and forms into their temples of democracy — the capitol buildings of their governments. The Greek Revolution sparked a revival of classical culture and architecture in New England. Carpenter handbooks became vehicles for spreading building styles throughout the country, and farmers shared their ideas through agricultural journals. All of these elements contributed to the popularity of Greek Revival architecture. By the 1830s, it was the most popular style in most areas of the country. As it spread to different regions, it took on distinctive characteristics. In some areas, climate would dictate certain characteristics; in others, available building materials would contribute to certain trends; and in still others, preferences for particular building and/or site orientations would distinguish the style. When Greek Revival style reached Oregon, it would display a wide variety of appearances, because all of the regions would be represented.

3

The Style Spreads

Alvin T. Smith informed us, by way of his diary and letters, that he lived in Connecticut and Illinois before he settled in Oregon. Most Oregonians did not leave records of their prior residences. For these individuals, census data are valuable resources for tracking settlement patterns. Traditionally scholars have used these records to develop theories about regionalism, politics, society, and culture. But by analyzing the birthplaces of individual family members in the census manuscripts, one can track the migration routes as well as the former residences of most immigrants.

The Jesse Looney family, listed in the 1850 Oregon census, illustrates how these data can serve as immigration tracking devices. The Looneys lived in at least six states or territories before arriving in Oregon. The father was born in Tennessee and the mother in Kentucky. They met and were married in Alabama, then moved to Wisconsin where their first child was born. Four years later, the family went to Illinois. From there, they migrated to Missouri, then on to Oregon in 1843. The Looneys had at least ten children by 1850, all within one to five years apart in age. The census listed the name, date, and place of birth for each child. By correlating the ages and birthplaces of each child, one can determine the family's migration pattern.[1] There is, however, at least one notable flaw in using census data to track migration patterns, and Alvin T. Smith illustrates the problem. He did not have any children, so the census record would not — and in fact did not — indicate that he had lived in Illinois.

Over forty years ago, historian Jesse Douglas studied the 1850 Oregon census, analyzing the origins of its inhabitants on a state-by-state basis. Although recent studies of the census are more comprehensive, Douglas's investigation offers the most useful material for the present inquiry.[2] Douglas counted about 12,000 individuals in Oregon in 1850, and he computed the number of males, females, and dependents from each state. For instance, he found that 2,291 pioneers came from Missouri, but of that number, 1,739 or 76 percent were children. On the other hand, the New England states provided 556 emigrants, but only 44 were children. In real numbers, 552 Oregon adults came from Missouri and 512 from New England. Although New Englanders did not make a substantial contribution to Oregon's population in terms of numbers, the large number of adults, as compared to children, suggests that the Northeast had a greater impact on Oregon's cultural background than numbers alone would indicate. Still, raw numbers are not always reliable. Many adults from the East and South were, themselves, children when they left their home states. Thus their cultural heritage was formed along the way to Oregon, which, in most cases, was in the Midwest. If census data are reliable, Greek Revival houses in Oregon should be similar to structures in the Midwest, and, to a lesser extent, buildings in the East and South.[3]

Identical Greek Revival houses were extremely rare. Even residences designed and built by the same carpenter in the same town seldom were alike. There were, however, particular characteristics that distinguished Greek Revival houses in one region from another, variations that reflected the environmental differences between regions and the familiarity of carpenters with particular building types. In the forested regions, builders used the local lumber supply for building houses. On the Great Plains, brick or stone became the primary building material, and in the arid Southwest, several adobe houses were decorated with classical detailing.

In the Northeast, the temple form was the most common house type. On some structures, porticoes created full temple fronts; on others, a simple porch took the place of a portico; and on still others, there was neither a portico nor a porch, and the pediment formed by the gable was the only evidence of style. In addition, a number of I-house, Georgian, and two-thirds Georgian type Greek Revival houses were constructed in the Northeast as well. Examples of northeastern Greek Revival architecture were discussed in the previous chapter.

In the antebellum South, the socioeconomic status of the house owner was an additional element in the selection of a house plan. Plantation mansions belonging to the landed gentry usually were Georgian type structures. The Georgian plan generally was square or nearly square in shape and three or, in some cases, five bays wide. In southern towns and cities, the Greek Revival style was popular among the middle-class merchants and professionals. These houses were

Georgian or two-thirds Georgian in some towns, temple form in others, and I-house type in still others. In the Midwest, temple form predominated in the north, while I-houses or bent-houses were the type chosen in the south. Sprinkled in both areas were a number of Georgian plan houses. In several Midwest enclaves, I-house plan structures featured full porticoes placed in the center of the front facade and perpendicular to the gable ends.[4]

In temple form houses, the gable ends are oriented toward the front and back, like a Greek temple. I-houses, quite simply, are shaped like the letter I. An I-house and temple form house differ by their entrance orientation; on the I-house, the front is placed on the longitudinal side. Bent-houses consist of a main block — often an I-house — with at least one wing projecting off at a perpendicular angle. A Georgian house is cubular in shape, with a central stairway. A two-thirds Georgian house, as the name suggests is two thirds of a Georgian house — more precisely the Georgian house narrowed in size, with a side hall, to make a row house.

GREEK REVIVAL ARCHITECTURE IN THE SOUTH

Greek Revival architecture crossed the Appalachians not long after William Strickland completed his Second Bank in Philadelphia. In fact, the bearer of the Greek Revival torch was Gideon Shryock, an architect who had apprenticed under Strickland. Shryock established an architectural office in Lexington, Kentucky, in 1824.[5] Three years after Shryock settled in Kentucky, he entered and won a contest to design the new statehouse in Frankfort. Shryock's plans called for a structure with a Greek temple front and Ionic columns supporting the portico; however, during the course of construction, he added a lantern cupola at the request of the capitol commissioners (Figure 3.1). The statehouse was finished in two years, the principal labor force consisting of inmates from the state penitentiary. At the completion of the project in 1829, Kentucky could boast one of the first classical buildings west of the Appalachians and the only Greek Revival statehouse in the country.[6]

In 1830, after the completion of his statehouse, Shryock designed Morrison Chapel at Transylvania College in Lexington; in 1833 he planned the county courthouse in Frankfort; and in 1835 he moved to Louisville where he was the architect for several other buildings. Throughout his career Shryock kept abreast of the recent trends in revival architecture. He adapted an interior doorway from Lafever's

Figure 3.1: Kentucky Statehouse, Frankfort, Kentucky. Designed by Gideon Shryock, 1829. *Photo by Kalman Papp.*

The Beauties of Modern Architecture into the main entrance of his Bank of Louisville.[7] Shryock's polished designs served as models for other classical structures in the Bluegrass State.

Kentucky provided 8 percent of Oregon's 1850 population, the largest number of immigrants in Oregon from any southern state. (The South as a whole represented 17 percent of its population in 1850.[8]) The tasteful designs of Shryock and others were influential on Oregon's classical dwellings. In particular, Oregon's larger Greek Revival houses traced their roots to southern plantation mansions.

Greek Revival was a practical style for southern plantation houses. The typical surrounding portico not only gave these structures the appearance of grandiose proportions, it also protected the superstructure from heavy rains and provided shade and cooling breezes through the large windows and doors in the main body of the house (Figure 3.2). Plantation mansions were so prevelant in the South before the Civil War, some northern visitors found them to be monotonous. As James Fennimore Cooper wrote in 1838:

Figure 3.2: Jean Pierre Emmanuel Prud'homme House, Natchitoches vicinity, Louisiana, ca. 1845. *Courtesy Louisiana Division of Historic Preservation.*

One such temple well placed in a wood might be a pleasant object enough, but to see a river lined with them, with children trundling hoops before their doors, beef carried into their kitchens, and smoke issuing, moreover, from those unclassical objects, is too much even for a high taste.[9]

Greek Revival architecture in the South generally is equated with Arlington House, the Hermitage, and other such elegant plantation manors. When southern cities profited from the cotton boom, however, their residents also built classical houses. Cities such as Charleston, South Carolina, Savannah, Georgia, New Orleans, Louisiana, and Richmond, Virginia, shared in the rich trade of "King Cotton," and each had large collections of Greek Revival houses.

Richmond was an interesting and unusual example of a developing city in the antebellum South. In addition to the cotton and tobacco industries, it was also an iron manufacturing and railroad center. The city had a fine collection of Greek Revival houses. For example, the William Beers house, constructed in 1839, was more restrained in detailing and amenities than most rural manors (Figure 3.3). It was a

Figure 3.3: William Beers House, Richmond, Virginia. Unknown builder, 1839. *Courtesy Virginia Department of Historic Resources.*

two-story brick structure with a low hipped roof, a bracketed cornice (which may have been added later), and a modest porch with two Doric support columns.[10] Tobacco merchant Anderson Barrett's house featured a stucco finish, a one-story Ionic portico on the exterior, and an elegant classical interior (Figure 3.4).[11]

GREEK REVIVAL ARCHITECTURE IN THE MIDWEST

Stylistically, as Greek Revival architecture spread through the Midwest, it was common for pilasters to replace formal columns, for simple architrave moldings or boxed cornices to suffice for entablatures, and for pediments to be represented by returns at the eaves. The doorway often served as a major focal point with surrounding decorative pilasters and entablatures.

Midwest pioneers from Missouri, Ohio, Illinois, Indiana, Iowa, Wisconsin, and Michigan represented 59 percent of Oregon's 1850 population. About 10 percent of all Oregonians came from Ohio.[12] Of Ohio's emigrants, 65 percent were adults. Included in this group of adults were thirty-two carpenters — the largest contingent from any state. From the examples of classical architecture in Oregon, it appears that at least some Ohio craftsmen were familiar with the Greek Revival houses in their native state.

Ohio was one of the first midwestern states to adopt classical architecture, and it did so in a big way. In most Ohio communities, buildings designed by architects and carpenters presented an appealing diversity. Many craftsmen possessed copies of the architectural pattern books by Benjamin, Lafever, and others, and they blended ideas from these sources into their designs. Architectural historian I. T. Frary has studied the local builders and their work in Ohio. Two houses in Chagrin Falls are of note here, one of which appeared to have no foundation and was placed on top of a hill, while the other stood on an unusually high basement in a valley. If the sites were switched, the structure on the hill would appear to be on stilts and the other would look as if it were submerged in mud. Vernacular house carpenters developed their own techniques for taking full advantage of their building sites.[13]

Zeno Kent was one of the earliest craftsmen to work in the classical style in Ohio. In fact, Kent started so early that his designs included a number of earlier colonial features. His oldest surviving structure is the house he built for his family in 1821. Although the residence had a Greek Revival flavor with a boxed cornice, eave returns on the gable

Figure 3.4: Anderson Barrett House, Richmond, Virginia. Unknown builder, ca. 1835. *Courtesy Virginia Department of Historic Resources*.

Figure 3.5: Joshua Giddings Law Office, Jefferson City, Ohio. Unknown builder, 1823. *Courtesy Historic America Building Survey.*

ends, and Doric pilasters on the front, the inclusion of a sunburst on the front door panel and much of the interior detailing gave the house a colonial, or Adamesque, appearance. Kent may have constructed the Judge Eben Newton house in nearby Mahoning County as well. Both residences shared similar detailing — a mixture of colonial and classical — both were within about ten miles of each other, and both were built about the same time.[14]

Later Ohio craftsmen studiously incorporated Lafever's plates into their work. Two houses near Wellington and one in Ashland provide an interesting sample. Since these towns were only twenty-five miles apart, it is conceivable that one man designed and built all three structures. For the two Wellington cottages, the carpenter used a classical example for the zigzag fret work design on the frieze; then he used an anthemion motif from Lafever's *Modern Builder's Guide* (plate 87) for the pilasters flanking the front door. On the Ashland residence, the designer borrowed the Lafever motif on the corner pilasters.[15]

Figure 3.6: Lane County Clerk's Office, Eugene, Oregon. Unknown builder, ca. 1853. *Courtesy Oregon State Parks.*

Classical commercial architecture also arrived in Ohio at an early date. Built in 1823, the Joshua Giddings Law Office in Jefferson City was the oldest Greek Revival office structure in the state (Figure 3.5). It has been preserved as a monument to the famous antislavery congressman who served his district with distinction for several decades before the Civil War. In the absence of a front portico, the doorway became the focal point for the Greek vocabulary. Doric pilasters capped with a full entablature surrounded the doorway, and a pediment over the entrance added to its templelike appearance. To save space and perhaps to draw attention to the detailing, the designer placed the doorway to the right of center.[16]

The Giddings Law Office was a modest and functional professional building. The design was similar for other offices throughout the Midwest and West. For example, a Kuchel and Dresel lithograph for Portland, Oregon, published in 1858, shows several small commercial buildings similar to the Giddings office in style and scale.[17] Today the Lane County Clerk's Office (ca. 1853) in Eugene is the only extant small Greek Revival office building in Oregon (Figure 3.6). Although the detailing and proportions are similar to the Ohio example, the

Figure 3.7: Sandusky County Courthouse, Fremont, Ohio. Designed by Mr. Williams, 1840. *Courtesy Historic American Building Survey, Library of Congress.*

builder of this structure used symmetrical fenestration on the front facade.[18]

As industry developed in Ohio, many companies constructed housing for the workers. In 1835 the Mad River and Lake Erie Railroad began building a line from Sandusky to Springfield, and by 1840 the track extended thirty miles south of Lake Erie. With its location at the head of the rail line, Sandusky became the hub for the east-west and north-south lines, thereby creating an employment boom.[19] The area's growth as a railroad center strengthened the economic base of Sandusky County. In 1839 its citizens began raising funds for a new courthouse in Fremont (Figure 3.7). One year later, having acquired the $14,500 necessary for the structure, the county hired a Mr. Williams as the architect and building superintendent. Williams was instructed to plan an inexpensive structure that would satisfy the needs of a

Figure 3.8: Lake County Courthouse, Paynesville, Ohio. Unknown builder, 1838. *Courtesy National Park Service.*

growing community. He responded with a Greek Revival courthouse that included a traditional Doric portico and an Ionic cupola. He parted from the typical classical design, though, by including a low-pitched hip roof in place of the traditional gabled pediment and a plain and unusually wide frieze in the place of an entablature.[20]

Sandusky was one of several counties that built a new courthouse. Lake County built a Greek Revival courthouse in Paynesville in 1838 (Figure 3.8), Knox County constructed a fine classical building in 1855, and Montgomery County built one of the most expensive and elaborate structures in the state in 1847 (Figure 3.9).[21] The Montgomery county commissioners hired Howard Daniels from Cincinnati to design the new courthouse in Dayton. A local legend states that Daniels attempted to copy faithfully the temple of Hephaestus (the Theseum) in Athens from an engraving in the possession of a local merchant. If the story is true, either the engraving was incorrect or Daniels used the Ionic rather than the Doric order on which the Theseum was based. White limestone was the primary building material, Ionic columns supported the front portico, and the entire edifice was surrounded by

Figure 3.9: Montgomery County Courthouse, Dayton, Ohio. Designed by Howard Daniels, 1847. *Courtesy National Park Service.*

a full and complete Ionic entablature. The Montgomery County Court-house cost $100,000, giving the city and county one of the most stunning Greek Revival structures in Ohio.[22]

Many Ohio churches were constructed in the classical style. Elegant cathedrals, such as St. Peter-In-Chains in Cincinnati (1841–45), were designed by professional architects in an attempt to rival the elegant ecclesiastical structures on the East Coast.[23] More common were the small-town churches scattered throughout the state. Like the Ohio houses and courthouses, most of these churches were planned and built by local carpenters, and the variations further contributed to the vernacular phase of Greek Revival architecture.

Of the Ohio churches, the Freewill Baptist Church in Colebrook is an interesting carpenter-designed example (Figure 3.10). In 1845 the Colebrook congregation built this fine Greek Revival meeting house. On the exterior, the designer created a dramatic effect by repeating classical elements on the various structural components. The entablature was prominent in its traditional location under the eaves, then the same motif was carried to the raking cornice of the pediments and as a

Figure 3.10: Freewill Baptist Church, Colebrook, Ohio. Unknown designer, 1845. *Courtesy Historic American Building Survey.*

formal cap over the entrance and on the cupola cornice. Four large Doric pilasters divided the front facade into three bays. Smaller pilasters, identical in style, decorated the corners of the cupola and flanked the doorway.[24] Although this building was relatively inexpensive, the restrained symmetry throughout and the repetitive use of details made this church one of the most tasteful classical structures in Ohio. Thus the Freewill Baptists proved that a building need not be expensive to be appealing.

Although no exact replicas of Ohio's Greek Revival structures appeared in Oregon, similar detailing and building components suggest that many transplanted Ohio carpenters built classical houses in their home state. In both states, wood was a prevalent construction material. In many cases, craftsmen experimented with their own interpretations of Greek Revival architecture, such as substituting pilasters for columns. Many Oregonians lived in or traveled through Ohio on

Figure 3.11: Second State Bank, Vincennes, Indiana. Designed by John Moore, 1838. *Courtesy Old State Bank State Historic Site.*

their way to the West. In short, the number of carpenters and settlers and the similarity of classical buildings are strong indications that Ohioans carried their architectural heritage with them to Oregon.

Oregon's 1850 population included a representation of about 8 percent from Indiana, 46 percent of which was adult. Although similarities between Greek Revival structures in Oregon and Indiana can be found, the stylistic relationship was not as strong as that between Oregon and Ohio. Greek Revival architecture appeared in Indiana during the 1820s; however, in 1832, Town and Davis's Indiana State Capitol provided a grand entrance for the style.

While the statehouse was under construction, the Second State Bank of Indiana was in the process of hiring a local craftsman, Edwin J. Peck, to construct a new branch building in Terre Haute. The directors perhaps were intrigued by the several Second Bank of the United States branch buildings across the country, for their branches were similar in style and scale.[25] Peck designed a banking room that consisted of a vaulted dome and skylight. On the exterior, Peck recreated the basic features of a Greek temple. A portico with four Doric columns, an entablature, and a pediment were typical for commercial buildings during this period. Yet the detail on the entablature frieze with triglyphs and metopes was striking and unusual.[26]

In 1834 the Second State Bank started another branch in Vincennes (fifty miles south of Terre Haute). In 1838 the board of directors hired John Moore to prepare plans for a permanent structure (Figure 3.11). Vincennes was in one of the earliest settled areas of the state, and Moore's design reflected the setting. The entire structure was brick, but the facade and the portico columns were covered with plaster to give the appearance of marble. Among the most novel features were the "Traders and Trappers Room" at the back of the building, which provided service to the less affluent customers, and a hidden room in the attic, designed to house a military garrison in the event of an invasion or civil insurrection.[27]

Stylistic bank buildings were symbols of economic expansion, although not necessarily prosperity. In 1838 the Indiana legislature encouraged development by enacting an ambitious internal improvements program, including the construction of a comprehensive canal system. The state borrowed over $6 million from the Second State Bank and other banks to fund the program, and by the mid-1840s, 179 miles of canals crisscrossed the commonwealth. The scheme was a monumental failure. Not only did the Panic of 1837 decimate financial institutions throughout the Midwest, but the introduction of railroads into the area demonstrated that rail service offered a more efficient and reliable transportation network.[28] When the state canal program failed, the Whitewater Company and several private corporations completed some of the projects. For its headquarters, the Whitewater firm constructed a Greek Revival building in Connersville in 1842 (Figure 3.12). The design was typical of other classical structures in Indiana with four Doric columns and a full entablature; however, the plan also included an unusual second story balcony inside the portico.[29]

During the 1840s and 1850s Indiana counties built new Greek Revival courthouses, similar in style to those in neighboring Ohio. The St. Joseph County Courthouse in South Bend (1853–55) was the showpiece of these new public buildings (Figure 3.13). The county commissioners hired architect John M. Van Osdel, who had designed a number of important structures in Chicago and elsewhere. Van Osdel copied many features from his earlier Cook County Courthouse in Chicago but varied the traditional Greek symmetry by unevenly placing the six columns on the portico. By using this technique, he broke

Figure 3.12: Canal House, Connersville, Indiana. Unknown designer, 1842. *Courtesy National Park Service.*

the monotony of even spacing between the support members and provided more visual exposure for the capped semicircular windows on the second story. Van Osdel incorporated the Corinthian order in the detailing, including the work on the elaborate cupola. Although the South Bend courthouse was definitely Greek Revival in style, certain elements on the window detailing and the cupola anticipated the Italianate style that was beginning to spread into the Midwest.[30]

Today it is difficult to realize that Chicago was not always the

Figure 3.13: St. Joseph County Courthouse, South Bend, Indiana. Designed by John M. Van Osdel, 1855. *Courtesy Northern Indiana Historical Society.*

largest city in Illinois. From the early 1800s until about 1830, Shawnee-town, in the southern part of the state, was the most prosperous and populous town. In 1821 Shawneetown boasted only thirty houses, two banks, and a United States land office. As the town grew, the Bank of Illinois kept pace, and by 1839 the board of directors decided to con-struct a new building.[31] The designer knew that Shawneetown was subject to the periodic flooding of the Ohio River, so he placed the edifice on an unusually high sandstone pedestal (Figure 3.14). In addi-tion to flood protection, the high base gave the structure a monumen-tal appearance, similar to the temples in ancient Greece. Also, the architect varied the spacing between the pillars by slightly tilting the two end columns about one inch toward the center. From a distance, the portico appeared to be perfectly symmetrical, whereas without the spacing, the tops of the columns would have appeared to tilt out-ward.[32]

The high base and the spacing on the portico suggest that the architect was familiar with classical concepts of design — except, for some reason, he placed five pillars on the portico rather than a tradi-tional even number. An interesting variation in the Greek Revival

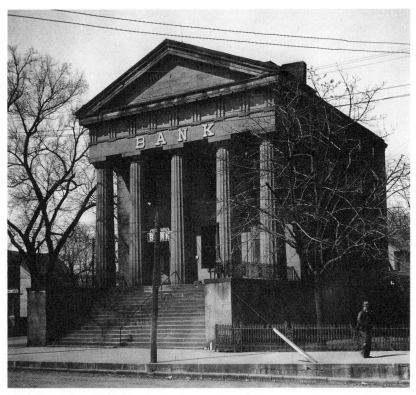

Figure 3.14: Bank of Illinois, Shawneetown, Illinois. Unknown designer, 1839. *Courtesy Historic American Building Survey.*

style, this treatment seemed to have a practical purpose. Two entrances were asymmetrically placed on the front facade, one for the banking room and the other leading to the second floor offices. With an odd number of columns, the doorways presented a well-placed appearance; an even number of pillars would have caused the entire front to appear unbalanced.[33]

By the 1840s Shawneetown and southern Illinois were bypassed economically and demographically. First, lead sulphide mines near Galena transferred the state's economic base to its northern part; then the portage route between the Great Lakes and the Mississippi River led to Chicago's predominance.[34] With this increased development, counties multiplied and classical courthouses were built in some of the new county seats. The structure in Henderson County provides a good example. In 1844 two local businessmen in Oquawka, the county seat,

Figure 3.15: Henderson County Courthouse, Oquawka, Illinois. Built by Alexis Phelps, 1844. *Courtesy Historic American Building Survey.*

Figure 3.16: Joseph Hoge House, Galena, Illinois. Designed by H. J. Stoefer, ca. 1845. *Courtesy Historic American Building Survey.*

donated land for the new courthouse and additional acreage to finance the new structure by the sale of lots. Although revenue from the land sale did not provide adequate funding for an elaborate building, local citizens still wanted a structure that would conform to the latest architectural style. Alexis Phelps was awarded a construction contract of $1,219 to build the courthouse. The completed building was small and vernacular (Figure 3.15). Four plain brick Doric columns, without a plaster coating, supported the portico.[35] A simple entablature surrounded the structure, a plain pediment completed the temple format, and a cupola gave the building the proper governmental appearance.

Greek Revival residential architecture in Galena, Illinois, was distinctive because of the formal porticoes on most of the structures. The Joseph Hoge House was one of the earliest Greek Revival dwellings. It included a formal temple front with a Doric portico, a pediment, and a full entablature (Figure 3.16). The designer and builder, H. J. Stoefer, came to Illinois from St. Louis and brought a familiarity of classical

Figure 3.17: Ann F. Telford House, Galena, Illinois. Unknown designer, ca. 1848. *Courtesy Historic American Building Survey.*

detailing. But he was not given a free stylistic hand in the plan. Joseph Hoge, the owner, was a successful lawyer from Maryland who insisted on the inclusion of imposing brick parapets on the sides of the structure.[36] The structure is, nevertheless, an important historical artifact with its mixture of the traditional eastern colonial and the more modern classical midwestern style.

The Hoge House represents a wealthy residence in Galena. Yet the dwellings of the middle- or lower-income residents featured formal porticoes as well. The Ann F. Telford House is a representation of the latter. Mrs. Telford's nephew, a carpenter, probably designed and constructed the house for his aunt in about 1848 (Figure 3.17).[37] Architecturally, the structure was a simple classical interpretation with a portico and a box cornice to represent the entablature.

Another carpenter, John Swartout, built his temple form house in Waukegan in 1847 (Figure 3.18). Four fluted Doric columns supported the portico, an archeologically correct Doric entablature surrounded the structure, and carved pilasters enhanced the corners of the main structure. Inside, crafted panels and the fireplace moldings appear to

Figure 3.18: John Swartout House, Waukegan, Illinois. Built by John Swartout, 1847. *Courtesy Historic American Building Survey.*

Figure 3.19: Newton Farmhouse, Belvidere, Illinois. Unknown designer, ca. 1850. *Courtesy Historic American Building Survey.*

Figure 3.20: William B. Sappington House, Arrow Rock vicinity, Missouri. Unknown builder, 1845. *Courtesy Missouri Department of Natural Resources.*

be made from expensive hardwood, when in fact these features were fashioned from pine and textured with varnish to simulate oak.[38]

Illinois was predominantly rural throughout the mid-1800s, and the countryside was dotted with Greek Revival houses. The Newton Farmhouse (ca. 1850) in Belvidere was typical of rural Illinois residences (Figure 3.19). It stands out as a generic model for many of the Greek Revival houses that would appear in Oregon.[39] The Newton House was a bent-house, built on a T-plan with the parlor and bedrooms located in the two-story main structure and the living room, kitchen, pantry, and main bedroom in the T extension.[40]

Oregon Greek Revival houses, constructed in the 1850s, employed a similar building plan, except the design was usually L-shaped rather than T-shaped. In place of the formal portico common in the Galena residences, the Newton House was entered through a recessed porch in the T extension, and there was no front doorway in the main two-story block. Most Oregon residences had a secondary entrance in the L, and the formal entrance generally was situated in the center of the front facade. At the corners of the Newton Farmhouse in Illinois and on most Oregon residences, large pilasters with cyma reversa caps to emulate Doric capitals served as structural support and decoration.

Figure 3.21: Aull House, Lexington, Missouri. Unknown designer, ca. 1847. *Courtesy Historic American Building Survey.*

Also, for the midwestern and northwestern houses, an entablature surrounded the structure at the eaves, and returns at the eaves represented a pediment.[41]

Based on birthplace, Illinois and Missouri contributed the largest number of Oregon immigrants — 36 percent of the total population. Individually, Illinois represented 11 percent and Missouri 25 percent.

Figure 3.22: Captain John C. Ainsworth House, Oregon City, Oregon. Unknown designer, 1851. *Courtesy Oregon State Parks.*

Two residences in Missouri show a noteworthy contrast. The William B. Sappington House near Arrow Rock and the Aull House in Lexington were within fifty miles of each other and located near the center of the state. The Sappington House, built between 1843 and 1845, was an elaborate residence with a two-story front portico and Doric style columns supporting the first level and Ionic pillars on the second story (Figure 3.20). Also, the builder chose the Ionic order for the entablature and pediment.[42] None of the extant Greek Revival houses in Oregon resembled the Sappington House. On the other hand, the Aull House in Lexington, constructed in about 1847, was nearly identical to the Ainsworth House in Oregon City (Figures 3.21–3.22). The Aull House featured a temple front with a portico supported by four fluted Doric columns. A full entablature surrounded the dwelling, and a balcony on the second story was placed within the portico. The entrance was situated to the left of center and surrounded by pilasters, side and transom lights, and an entablature — identical in detailing to the larger entablature under the eaves.[43]

The Aull House was situated on a high bank in Lexington and located at the crossing of a major road between eastern and western Missouri and the Missouri River. At this location many Oregonians

Figure 3.23: Woodlawn, Smyrna, Delaware. Unknown designer, 1855. *Photo Robert K. Sutton.*

Figure 3.24: Sam Houston House, Huntsville, Texas. Unknown designer, ca. 1850. *Courtesy Texas Historical Commission.*

who had lived in Missouri or others traveling by land or water across the state probably saw the Aull House. Perhaps the strategic location of the Aull House explains its similarity to the Ainsworth house in Oregon City. The Missouri House was constructed of brick, and the Ainsworth residence of lumber; the entrance to the Oregon City House was on the right side of the front facade, the Aull house to the left. With the exception of these minor variations, the dwellings were nearly identical. Ainsworth was a riverboat pilot on the upper Mississippi River before he went west with the California gold rush in 1850. He may have seen the Aull House during his travels. More likely, the carpenter who constructed the Ainsworth residence may have noted the Missouri dwelling before emigrating to Oregon.[44]

HOUSES REMODELED TO GREEK REVIVAL STYLE

Greek Revival architecture spread throughout the Midwest, the East, and the South before 1850. The style was so popular, many house owners remodeled their residences to reflect the new building trend.

Figure 3.25: Sam Houston House, Huntsville, Texas. Unknown designer, ca. 1850. *Courtesy Texas Historical Commission*.

Some individuals added classical porticoes to existing fine houses. Others upgraded log cabins to Greek Revival dwellings by adding lumber siding and classical detailing. Woodlawn in Smyrna, Delaware, was such a structure (Figure 3.23). In its present appearance, the mansion features a magnificent portico with six fluted Doric columns, a full pediment, a generous entablature, and a handsomely detailed entrance. According to local tradition, Colonel George W. Cummins, an early owner, converted a plain Georgian type house to its present appearance in 1853. During the early 1970s, however, the owners were restoring the building and discovered that one of the walls was constructed of hewn logs. Thus Woodlawn probably was not always a large mansion. Part or all of it may have been a log cabin at one time.[45]

Fifteen hundred miles away another owner decided to convert his house into a classical residence. Sam Houston purchased a small parcel of land in 1847 at Huntsville, Texas. Within two years he had constructed a hewn log dogtrot cabin and purchased several adjoining parcels of land, giving him a total of 234 acres.[46] He referred to the site as a "bang-up place" and continued to remodel, adding a porch with

Figure 3.26: Sam Colver House, Phoenix, Oregon. Built by Sam Colver, 1852. *Courtesy Oregon State Parks.*

square Doric-like columns, a simple pediment, siding, and molding over the windows (Figures 3.24–3.25).[47] Houston's house was simple, without the traditional classical elements, such as an entablature. It was so simple, in fact, that the passage between both parts of the house (the dogtrot) was only partially enclosed. Lattice work over the doors on the front and back allowed breezes to flow through the dwelling.

Sam Colver, one of Sam Houston's Texas Rangers, left the Southwest in 1851 and went to Oregon. He and his family settled on a Donation Land Claim in Phoenix in the southern part of the territory.[48] When the Colvers arrived in the Rogue River Valley, their neighbors were embroiled in a war with the Umpqua and Rogue Indians. The new arrivals needed a house, and the other settlers wanted a fortress for protection against Indian attack. In 1852 the Colvers built a substantial hewn-log structure on their claim to serve both purposes. The timbers were fourteen inches thick with observation holes in the logs and three doors in the front of the structure. In 1853 the Rogue River Indian War ended with the Treaty of Table Rock, and the community no longer needed a fort. The Colvers continued to use the structure as a house. Some of the floor space became a hostelry and school, and the upper floor a meeting and social hall.[49]

Sometime during the late 1850s or early 1860s, Sam Colver covered his house with clapboards, built a two-story front portico, and decorated the eaves with a boxed cornice (Figure 3.26).[50] The conversion changed the structure into a vernacular Greek Revival house. Surviving documentation does not reveal when or why Colver remodeled the building. Other classical structures were erected in the area by the 1860s, and perhaps he liked the style and decided to alter his residence to keep up with the times. Also, gold was discovered in nearby Jacksonville in the early 1850s, and perhaps Colver improved his financial lot from the mines and could afford to add siding. Colver's house was an unusual example of Greek Revival architecture in Oregon. Most classical house owners built entirely new residences to replace log cabins. Yet Colver and the others had some things in common. They copied a style that was popular throughout the country, and they invested their wealth in stylish residences.

4

The Settlement of Oregon

When Sam Colver settled in southern Oregon, his first priorities were to provide shelter for his family and protection for his neighbors during the Rogue River Indian War. He was not concerned about stylistic expression; he simply wanted to build a structure that would fulfill practical needs. Several years later, after he had developed his land claim and improved his financial situation, he upgraded his house by adding the clapboard siding and a portico.

SETTLING THE FRONTIER

Like Colver, Oregon pioneers usually did not build Greek Revival houses when they first arrived in the Pacific Northwest. In fact, relatively few Oregonians ever constructed classical houses, and for those who did there was a ten-to-fifteen-year lapse between the erection of the first shelter and a Greek Revival residence. Typically the early settler built a simple dwelling and started farming the land or establishing a business, dreaming of the time when he could construct a fancy new house. Some realized their dreams through frugality and hard work while acquiring more land. Yet a majority of the pioneers who built Greek Revival houses did so only after they benefited from the California gold rush. Oregon was a virtual wilderness in 1840, but ten years later there were about 12,000 inhabitants, several small industries, and a few elaborate houses with distinctive architectural detailing.

It seems only appropriate to begin this discussion with Alvin T. Smith. Although his diary typically was cryptic — usually not longer than one line — taken as a whole, the information it imparts is invaluable. In addition to Smith's recorded observations, other diaries and personal accounts have survived in manuscript or published form. These contemporary sources provide vivid portrayals of early Oregon life.

Before the pioneers settled in Oregon, they first had to make the strenuous trek across the plains. Although he was not the first to make the journey in a covered wagon, Smith was one of the earliest travelers to record his experiences. He was a deeply religious man, a member of the Congregational Church. Although not college or seminary trained, he decided to become a missionary to the Indians in the Pacific Northwest after attending a week-long series of religious services in Quincy, Illinois.[1]

When Smith and his bride left Quincy, they spent several weeks visiting friends as they traveled across Missouri on the way to their debarkation point at Westport. There they gathered supplies and traded mules until they had a compatible team. Later the Smiths joined the other members of the party — the Reverend and Mrs. Harvey Clark and Mr. and Mrs. Philo B. Littlejohn — and on 29 April 1840, they began their journey to Oregon.[2] Before departing, the party arranged to accompany American Fur Company traders going to the Green River (present-day Wyoming) where the spring rendezvous would take place. Their route took them along the Kansas River, then followed the Little Blue and Big Blue rivers (in Kansas) north until it reached the Platte River (Nebraska). They continued along the North Platte past Chimney Rock and the future site of Fort Laramie (Wyoming) to Independence Rock and Devil's Gate, then down the Sweetwater and Big Sandy rivers to the Green River. From there, the group proceeded without a guide until it reached Fort Hall (Idaho) on 20 July, where Smith traded his wagon to the Hudson's Bay Company in payment for transporting his goods (1,440 pounds) to Fort Walla Walla. The Americans continued their journey on horseback, reaching Fort Boise on 4 August and their final destination, the Whitman Mission at Waiilatpu (Washington), on 14 August.[3]

Smith and his wife spent about ten weeks at the Whitman Mission, where he helped construct several buildings, repair Dr. Whitman's adobe house, and harvest the wheat crop. For two weeks in September the Smiths traveled in the northeastern Oregon country on an "exploring tour" with the Reverend and Mrs. J. S. Griffin.[4] They then packed their belongings and went to the Lapwai Mission on the Clearwater River (near present-day Lewiston, Idaho) to construct a sawmill for the Reverend Henry Harmon Spalding. Smith supervised the project from November until August 1841 when he and Mrs. Smith left to establish a mission school in the Willamette Valley. Shortly afterwards, Spalding wrote to the Reverend David Greene, secretary for the American Board of Commissions for Foreign Missions in Boston, saying of

Smith: "his kindness and patience and industrious habits and good judgement and ardent but consistent zeal, I have never seen combined in one man before."[5]

With the exception of the year spent at Waiilatpu and Lapwai, Smith's experience was much like that of other pioneers arriving in Oregon. He left the Missouri River in the spring after most of the rivers had receded following the spring runoff and when the prairies were sprouting grass to feed the livestock. The overland trip took about three-and-a-half months, and his party arrived in the Oregon country in the late summer. Like a large majority of immigrants, Smith was a farmer, which meant that he missed harvesting a crop the first year. He was, however, a skilled carpenter and found employment at the Whitman and Lapwai missions. Many pioneers did not have an additional skill and had to rely on their savings, credit from the Hudson's Bay Company at Fort Vancouver, or the kindness of neighbors to make it through their first year.

The Smiths reached the falls of the Willamette River at Oregon City on 22 September and settled on a land claim near present-day Forest Grove on 28 September. He purchased staples from local residents and started clearing his land within two days.[6] For the next two weeks, he worked "on the yard" and made preparations to build a house. The construction of a simple dwelling in that frontier setting was not an easy task even for a craftsman such as Smith. Sawn lumber was available from the Hudson's Bay Company at Fort Vancouver, but it was nearly impossible to transport this material to his land claim on the Tualatin Plains. In fact, it was difficult to carry heavy loads even for short distances because few Oregonians owned large wagons. Smith devised a system to haul timber from the nearby woods to his construction site by boring holes through the centers of log segments and using them as wheels. The improvised vehicle must have been awkward to load and difficult for a team of oxen to pull. The friction of the ungreased wooden wheels on the log axle must have made an almost unbearable screeching noise. Yet it did provide the needed mode of transportation. With the help of his strange-looking (and -sounding) contraption, Smith was able to fell and transport all of the necessary timber to his homestead within two weeks.[7]

Smith's description indicates that the house was a frame structure rather than a log cabin, but the detail he recorded is insufficient to indicate its appearance. He used the simple construction technique of placing sleepers (squared logs) on the ground for the foundation; then he framed the superstructure with adzed timbers. It took nearly two months for Smith to cut and split the siding used to cover the exterior and shingle the roof.[8] He continued working on his new dwelling through the winter and by March had completed the floor, the door, and some interior furniture. With his house essentially finished, Smith spent the rest of the spring clearing land, planting crops, and building fences to keep wild animals out of his garden.[9]

Smith did not build a Greek Revival house at first — in fact classical structures did not exist in Oregon at that time. There were, however, many substantial buildings in the Pacific Northwest when he arrived. Fort Vancouver, the headquarters for the Hudson's Bay Company's Columbia Department, consisted of twenty-one buildings surrounded by a stockade. Most of these structures were built with the "post-in-the-sill" technique. Square timbers made up the framing system, the sill beam served as the foundation, and the vertical and horizontal members made up the framing system.[10] Perhaps Smith constructed his house using the "post-in-the-sill" method. He framed the dwelling with hewn timbers, but also covered the exterior with clapboards — not a common treatment for this type of structure. In addition to Fort Vancouver, the Hudson's Bay Company operated a chain of trading posts throughout the Oregon country. Most of these forts were similar to the buildings at Fort Vancouver, but in the dry climates east of the Cascades Mountains, some posts were adobe.[11]

The Hudson's Bay Company was the dominant force in the Pacific Northwest from the 1820s through the early 1840s. By the early 1830s, however, several small mission complexes were beginning to make their impact on the region. Dr. Marcus Whitman's mission compound at Waiilatpu, where Smith spent his first two months in Oregon, was constructed with adobe bricks placed within a pegged timber frame. Henry Spalding's Lapwai Mission included structures that were built with a variety of techniques. Some were "post-in-the-sill" structures, others were framed adobe similar to Whitman's buildings, and still others were hewn-log cabins. At least one of Spalding's structures exhibited the medieval "waddle-and-dab" method of a frame interwoven with thin saplings and covered with a smooth mud plaster finish. The Reverend Jason Lee developed his Methodist Mission in the Willamette Valley near Salem with framed clapboard structures. These buildings were devoid of stylistic detailing, resembling simple New England "salt-box" houses in form.[12]

Although a skilled carpenter, Smith did not have the proper tools, hardware, and equipment, and it took him several months to construct a simple house. Many immigrants arriving in Oregon lacked Smith's carpentry talents as well as the necessary funds to hire a professional house builder. Thus, it became a common practice for newcomers to construct crude log cabins to provide basic shelter. Basil N. Longsworth, an 1853 pioneer, later described the process of building such a structure:

> Yesterday he [his brother James Edward] took possession of his claim and today we went to work on it and cut poles and built a little pen 10 feet square[,] made boards and covered it and moved into it — baked hot biscuits for supper and did all this before dark, at which time the rain commenced falling quite fast and continued so all night, but the roof turned water well and we were dry — warm and merry.[13]

John Minto, an 1844 arrival, mentioned that he and two friends worked for a contractor for several weeks building simple log cabins on the Tualatin Plains. The Oregon Provisional Government Code, passed in 1843, allowed pioneers to acquire 640 acres of land if the claimant improved the land within six months and resided on it within a year. Also, settlers were required to construct houses sixteen feet square and six feet from the ground to the eaves. Minto and his co-workers built five such houses in six days and many more similar structures during the remainder of their employment.[14]

Since the incoming settlers often had either expended their financial resources on the journey or were anxious to start working on their land claims, most were satisfied to live in a simple shelter. As the population increased, some of the newcomers had the means to live in something more substantial than a log cabin. Philip Foster sailed to Oregon in 1843 with a supply of goods to establish a dry goods and hardware business in Oregon City. Within a short time he constructed a three-story building for his residence and store, and he wrote that property values in Oregon City had increased more than 300 percent since his arrival eight months earlier. Foster's business was successful, but he also recognized the advantages for skilled craftsmen in Oregon City. He and Walter Pomeroy signed an agreement with Dr. John McLoughlin of the Hudson's Bay Company to build a mill at the falls of the Willamette River. Within four months after they started the mill, Foster and Pomeroy accepted Jacob Wain as a partner and expanded the business to include house construction. From October 1843 through 1844, the partners built the mill and nine individual residences, employing as many as fifteen workers at one time. They erected everything from small frame dwellings to a large house for A. E. Wilson in Oregon City at a cost of $533.25.[15]

The houses Foster and his partners constructed were not unusual in Oregon City, but the farmers living away from the towns could only dream of having frame and sawn-lumber houses. Some rural inhabitants continued to live in their crude shelters for several years. For most pioneers, however, the simple log cabin was only temporary, and within months or a few years, they began building more permanent hewn-log houses. For example, Basil N. Longsworth began cutting and squaring timbers for a new house within a week after he built the first shelter, and in three months he had completed and moved into the hewn-log dwelling. Typically, a farming family lived in the more permanent log houses for several years, then built frame houses, which in some cases were Greek Revival.[16] Or, the hewn-log cabin might fulfill the needs of other Oregonians, and they did not build a frame house.

Sam Colver remained in his large timber residence in Phoenix, but he made it more stylistic by adding classical detailing. Thirty-five miles to the north, near the community of Rogue River, David Birdseye constructed a one-and-a-half-story hewn-log house in 1856 (Figure 4.1). Birdseye may have taken timbers from an abandoned fort used during the Rogue River Indian War, or cut and squared the logs himself from a nearby stand of pine trees. Whatever the case, the well-built cabin has survived for over a century and is still occupied by his descendants.[17]

In the northern part of the territory, Horace Baker erected a hewn-log house near Carver in 1856 with an unusual cantilevered roof and an exterior stairway leading to the second floor (Figure 4.2).[18] Both Birdseye and Baker were content to make their log structures permanent dwellings, which in part explains their survival. In contrast, John Stauffer built a squared-log residence in Aurora Colony in 1864 with expertly crafted dovetail corner joints. This structure has survived longer than the 1885 frame and lumber house he built to replace the original cabin.[19]

For Basil Longsworth, Alvin Smith, and the typical Oregon pioneer, a crude dwelling was tolerable as a temporary shelter. Before building more comfortable residences, however, settlers usually constructed barns for storing their crops. Often a simple shed was adequate to protect the first crop, but in most cases, a permanent barn was

Figure 4.1: David Birdseye House, Rogue River, Oregon. Built by David Birdseye, 1856. *Courtesy Oregon State Parks.*

Figure 4.2: Horace Baker Cabin, Carver, Oregon. Built by Horace Baker, 1856. *Courtesy Oregon State Parks.*

a higher priority than a hewn-log house.[20] One visitor to the Oregon frontier in 1859 described this phenomenon:

> [I] rode 4 miles into the country this morning to see a person spoken of as a Friend [Quaker]. In a rude timber house . . . having no windows or light except when the door was open, we found Hiram Bond and wife, with a family of 9 children. They immigrated to this country about 11 years ago, having lived in Indiana and Iowa. Their farm consists of 640 acres of land which is mostly fenced in. They are putting up a large new barn, and I think a new house is wanting for their comfort.[21]

Alvin Smith's major construction project for 1843 was a new barn. He began hauling timber in January and did not finish the structure until February a year later. In August and September, Smith and his neighbors spent six days raising the main framework, and then he added the roof, covered it with siding, and laid the floor. Smith indicates in his diary that the new barn required even more effort and expertise than the mill he built for Spalding at Lapwai.[22]

During the 1840s, pioneers usually developed their farm buildings in a predictable fashion — log cabin, temporary barn, permanent barn, and hewn-log house. But in the towns, the availability of materials and expertise allowed the inhabitants to construct sawn-lumber houses. In 1845 Dr. McLoughlin began erecting a residence near his mill in Oregon City. Both buildings were completed in 1846, and McLoughlin left the Hudson's Bay Company to live in Oregon and operate his business. His new house was perhaps the most elaborate residence in Oregon at that time (Figure 4.3). It was reminiscent of an eighteenth-century New England or eastern Canadian I-house. It was framed and covered with weatherboarding and had neither distinguishing architectural detailing nor a front or rear porch.[23]

While Dr. McLoughlin's house and mill were under construction, Great Britain and the United States established their boundary at the forty-ninth parallel. Oregon City was inside American territory. As part of the Oregon Treaty, the Hudson's Bay Company maintained possessory rights to its property and business activities in American territory — including a store in Oregon City. Francis Ermatinger was appointed the Hudson's Bay Company manager in 1844 and about a year later built a house near the Willamette River. In general appearance, Ermatinger's residence was similar to McLoughlin's, except for a flat roof. In about ten years, this roof proved unsatisfactory in the

Figure 4.3: Dr. John McLoughlin House, Oregon City, Oregon. Unknown builder, 1845. *Courtesy Oregon State Parks.*

damp climate, and it was replaced with a more conventional hip roof.[24]

Although the Hudson's Bay Company maintained its rights on American soil, it gradually shifted its interests further north and moved its regional headquarters from Fort Vancouver to Fort Victoria in British Columbia. Instead of following the company to Canada, Dr. Forbes Barclay, the post surgeon, decided to establish a medical practice in Oregon City. He purchased a lot and arranged for a contractor to build a new house before he arrived in 1850. His new residence became the first known example of Greek Revival architecture in Oregon (Figure 4.4). Unfortunately, documentation has not survived that would indicate whether it was Barclay or his builder who selected the classical mode. The basic features characterizing the style, such as an entablature, pilasters on the corners, and molding around the doorway, were missing, but the porch was a simple representation of a portico with square columns topped with molded caps to suggest capitals. While much of the evidence is scanty, the price is well documented. Dr. Barclay paid about $17,000 for his residence — an enormous sum when compared to the Wilson House, which cost $533.25 in 1844.[25]

Figure 4.4: Dr. Forbes Barclay House, Oregon City, Oregon. Unknown builder, 1850. *Courtesy Oregon State Parks.*

CALIFORNIA GOLD RUSH

Barclay's dwelling was larger and much more stylistic than the Wilson House, but quality alone does not explain the cost differential. The *Oregon City Oregon Spectator* in its 16 August 1848 issue explained the reason. The brig *Louise* arrived in Oregon bringing the exciting news of the discovery of gold in California. According to the ship's crew, residents had abandoned California's coastal towns. Further, gold dust brought fifteen dollars an ounce in San Francisco, and laborers were refusing salaries of ten to fifteen dollars a day and heading for the goldfields. For the first time in the *Spectator's* history, an issue was soldout within hours. A week later the newspaper stated that Oregonians in great numbers were either preparing to go or had already left for California. The editor cautioned that the information from California almost certainly was exaggerated. Two weeks later another ship, the *Henry*, docked in Oregon City carrying a copy of the *San Francisco Californian* of 15 July. The *Spectator* printed excerpts saying that the digging started in May and the daily finds ranged from $10 to $350.[26]

For the next month, the Oregon City newspaper was not published, and on 17 October the editor gave this explanation:

> The gold fever which has swept about 3000 of the officers, lawyers, physicians, farmers, and mechanics from the plains of Oregon into the mines of California took away our printers also — hence the temporary nonappearance of the *Spectator.*

He concluded by stating that Oregon was still more desirable than California because of the long-term agricultural benefits provided by the fertile soil. Furthermore, the editor predicted the eventual discovery of gold in Oregon.[27]

Estimates place the Oregon population of 1848 at between ten and twelve thousand, with about four to five thousand adult males.[28] The *Spectator* stated that three thousand men had gone to the mines by October 1848, which, if true, left relatively few mature males in the territory. When the men went to California, the women stayed behind to take care of the farms and the children.[29] So many men departed from the Clatsop Plains near Astoria that cattle were left untended, resulting in a serious, unregulated overgrazing problem.[30] Sometimes single parents contracted with relatives or friends to care for their children while they sought their fortunes.[31] To many Oregonians, nevertheless, gold fever appeared as a crisis with no apparent relief. Mrs. Alvin T. Smith, who saw a moral and religious decline in her neighbors as a result of the affliction, wrote a friend in 1853:

> This glittering dust which so much excites and intoxicates the hearts of men not only in California and Oregon, but we may say the whole world . . . separates many families and has made shipwreck of many souls. It is enough to astound anyone to hear of so many falling from a religious character to infamy and ruin.[32]

Peter Burnett, an 1843 pioneer, was one of the first Oregonians to head south with a wagon. He had been a district attorney and farmer in Platte County, Missouri, and in Oregon continued to practice law as well as farm his 640-acre claim. Although dedicated to establishing an American territory in Oregon, he could not resist the lure of the gold rush and the dream of instant wealth. When Burnett decided to try his luck in the mines, many Oregonians had already left by ships or pack trains. He noticed that in their haste, his neighbors carried only enough food and clothing for the journey south, which would necessitate purchasing mining equipment and supplies in California. He correctly anticipated the expense of these items in the goldfields and concluded that he would meet with more success by carrying his provisions by wagon. Convincing a group of 150 men to join the venture, Burnett and his party left with fifty wagons under the direction of Thomas McKay, a former employee of the Hudson's Bay Company. When the expedition reached the Sacramento Valley in November, it was the first wagon train to travel between Oregon and California. Burnett, his brother-in-law, and a nephew bought and successfully mined a claim on the Yuba River, then returned to Oregon early the next spring to pay off debts and regale their friends with tales of their adventures. Later in 1849 Burnett returned to the diggings, but this time he stayed. The former Oregonian prospected for a time, became the administrator for John Sutter's vast landholdings, and was elected as California's first governor in 1850.[33]

After Burnett and his fellow gold seekers left Oregon, the *Spectator* observed that many farms and buildings had deteriorated, and that over three hundred Oregonians had died or were killed in their headlong dash for riches to the south. An editorial in 1850 concluded by stating:

> There is no mending these things [dead and deteriorated farms] now, but let us profit by it in the future, and keep the plow going, for in the earth of this entire valley and other valleys are large quantities of the hidden treasure. Stay away from the mines — let them go to grass.[34]

Many Oregonians took the *Spectator's* advice, remained at home, and succeeded handsomely from the general prosperity in Oregon. Before the gold rush, prices were stable and the barter system was a common means of selling goods and services. For example, in May 1847 Alvin T. Smith traded a horse to a local farmer for forty-five bushels of "good wheat" and five dollars in cash to be paid six months later.[35] Pork sold for four cents a pound, a cow and calf for about thirty-five dollars, fence rails for one dollar per one hundred lineal feet, and wheat for an average of about eighty cents a bushel. Common laborers hired out for about twenty dollars per month or four dollars per week.[36] By 1850, however, wheat was selling for $2.50 per bushel, pork for ten cents a pound, lumber for fifty to sixty dollars per thousand feet, cattle for fifty dollars a head, and beef for an average of nineteen cents a pound. Skilled workers received eight to ten dollars a day, and common laborers were paid four to five dollars per day.[37] Since most of the men were in California, job opportunities were plentiful.

In part, the inflated prices resulted from a scarcity of goods in Oregon. Residents in the Pacific Northwest relied on an annual shipment of supplies received at Fort Vancouver each year, and in 1848 the cargo on board the Hudson's Bay Company ship *Vancouver* was lost in a shipwreck at the mouth of the Columbia River. In addition, the ships that occasionally came to Oregon from the East sold their merchandise in San Francisco, then brought gold to the Northwest to exchange for lumber and produce.[38] Yet even though merchandise was scarce during 1848, the gold rush provided opportunities for those with enough money and entrepreneurial skill.

George Abernethy, provisional governor of Oregon and a former employee of Jason Lee's Willamette Mission, owned a lumber mill in Oregon City. With the discovery of gold, he initially was concerned that the lack of manpower would threaten his operation. He soon realized, however, that his mill was an asset that could bring him a great deal of money. By 1849 Abernethy's mill was operating around the clock, producing about 6,000 board feet of lumber a day. Because of the shortage of labor, he was forced to pay more than double the normal wages and freight costs to Portland. Yet Abernethy cleared an estimated $26,000 in 1849. Then, he sold his Oregon City interests for $35,000 and constructed a new mill at Oak Point on the Columbia River, which provided both a deep water anchorage and a large stand of timber adjacent to the site. With the remarkable profits from the lumber sold in California — $400 per thousand feet in November 1849 — he established a new partnership that included shipping to and from California and the East Coast.[39] The gold rush that made Oregon products desirable, and the aggressive marketing of such entrepreneurs as Abernethy, provided a steady flow of merchandise into and out of the Pacific Northwest by 1852.

Actually, the prices of almost all goods and services were inflated during the gold rush. In addition to the high cost of commodities and labor, land values skyrocketed during this period. Forty-five years later, Mrs. W. W. Buck recalled that she and her husband had paid $3,000 for a lot in Oregon City, $100 per thousand feet for lumber to build a new house, and eight dollars a day for carpenters to construct their building.[40]

Alvin T. Smith purchased two lots in the small town of Hillsboro (the county seat of Washington County) for $1,025 in 1850, as well as a one-third share in the steamer *Gold Hunter* for $1,000. Although Smith was not as ambitious as Abernethy, he fared quite well during this time. Before 1848 he and his wife had become self-sufficient by raising livestock, selling cash crops, and tending a large garden. In his diary, Smith indicates that he accumulated only a small amount of capital before the gold rush, but between 1849 and 1851 he made sizable profits. For example, early in 1850 he sold two oxen for $125, and one year later four oxen went for $525.[41]

Oregon's political system also suffered from the instability caused by the gold rush. From 1843 through 1848 Oregon was loosely governed by the provisional government. During this five-year period, there were several changes in the system. The three-man executive council was replaced by one governor (George Abernethy), and the legislative body included more members. The mandate under which the government operated, however, did not change. It provided law and order until the establishment of a permanent form of government. While most men were on their way to the goldfields, President James K. Polk signed a bill in August 1848 creating the Territory of Oregon. The provisions of the territorial act specified that the provisional government would continue to operate until a territorial governor and legislature were in office. Yet when the provisional legislative body was called into session late in 1848, only nine of its twenty-three members were present. The rest either had gone to California or had lost interest. Unable to conduct business, Governor Abernethy called for new elections, and a quorum of eighteen members finally convened on 5 February 1849.[42] Within a month, Joseph Lane arrived as the newly appointed territorial governor and the provisional legislature was abandoned.

Abernethy gradually withdrew from politics during the gold rush to concentrate on his various business enterprises. At the same time, other Oregonians who profited from the new economic order became more interested in politics. James W. Nesmith was elected as a supreme court justice under the provisional government in 1845. During the time he held this position, he built a gristmill in the community of Rickreall (near Salem) in about 1848. His timing was perfect and he was enormously successful, selling flour to the California miners for twenty-five dollars a barrel. With this new-found wealth, Nesmith built a fine Greek Revival house in Rickreall in 1855 (Figure 4.5).[43] During the 1850s, he remained active in politics and eventually was elected as one of the Oregon's first United States senators in 1859.

Many Oregon businessmen achieved prosperity from a variety of activities. For example, Jacob Spores came to Oregon in 1847 with his wife and seventeen children and settled on a claim north of the McKenzie River near Eugene. Shortly after his arrival, Spores solicited the aid of local Indians to build a log cabin and a ferry across the McKenzie.[44] When the mass exodus to the California diggings began in 1848,

Figure 4.5: James W. Nesmith House, Rickreall, Oregon. Unknown designer, 1855. *Courtesy Oregon State Parks.*

large numbers of travelers required the services of Spores's ferry to cross the river. No record has survived that would indicate his earnings from the ferry, but the law of supply (this was the only easy crossing) and demand (the miners were in a hurry) would suggest that he made sizable profits from his operation. While earnings at the river crossing can only be hypothesized, the figures from his farm are available. The editor of the *Spectator* selected Spores's farm as an example to demonstrate the profitability of Oregon agriculture in 1850, saying:

> I know Jacob Spores of Linn [later Lane] County had 55 acres of wheat last year which to say the least would yield 25 bushels to the acre. The wheat was all harvested. It would yield 5 bushels per barrel, 250 barrels of flour. This at $14 per barrel would be worth $3,500.[45]

With his combined income, Spores constructed a new Greek Revival house on his claim in about 1854.[46]

While many Oregonians prospered during the California gold rush, for those on limited or fixed incomes the inflated prices brought new hardships. For example, the Elkanah Walker family came to the Oregon Country in 1838 to establish a mission at Tshimakain near Spokane. They served as missionaries until the Whitman Massacre in 1848 and then moved to Oregon City. After their ten years as missionaries, with a meagre income, the Walkers were nearly destitute when they arrived in Oregon. Yet friends in Oregon City provided assistance, and with borrowed money and several months of hard work, they bought a house for $3,000. After a year, they moved to Forest Grove, purchased a farm, and sold the house in Oregon City for about twice the purchase price. In 1851 the farm was returned to its original owner over a disputed title, and the Walkers were left without property or money.[47] Mrs. Walker later reported to her longtime friend, Myron Eells, that the loss of the farm, the absence of steady income, and the inflation caused by the California gold rush made the years between 1849 and 1852 the most difficult of her life.[48]

With the attraction of gold in California, immigration to Oregon decreased to only 450 in 1849, the smallest number since 1843. But the next year, the number increased dramatically to 6,000 settlers — more than any single year to that time.[49] Oregon's fertile land continued to hold an attraction for farmers. Further, word reached the East that many prospectors had been unsuccessful. As settlers again headed for Oregon, a legend developed that indicated Oregonians were concerned about the quality of the new pioneers who soon would be joining them:

> At Pacific Springs, one of the crossroads of the western trail, a pile of gold bearing quartz marked the road to California; the other road had a sign bearing the words "To Oregon." Those who could read took the trail to Oregon.[50]

Despite this myth, newcomers often came to Oregon after first going to California and trying their luck at mining.[51] Undoubtedly, many of these immigrants originally intended to head for Oregon; they could not resist the attraction of potential wealth, however, and made a detour to the goldfields. One family took a rather circuitous route to the Willamette Valley. William Sperry left his farm in Missouri in 1849 for the goldfields. Although he did not make a fortune, he was moderately successful and returned to his Missouri farm the next spring. Within a year, he was on the move again, but this time he took his entire family to Oregon. Sperry was a Baptist minister, and although he did not explain why he chose Oregon over California, it seems safe to assume that he thought the Pacific Northwest a more desirable place than California to raise children. Indeed, his clan was a major concern, for he had twelve children, and several of his offspring had families of their own. The Sperrys departed in April 1851 — three weeks after the birth of a daughter — with five wagons and about two hundred head of livestock.[52] After they arrived, the entire family settled near Brownsville, and Sperry built a house that was a very crude representation of classical revival architecture. Sperry died in 1857, but not before founding two Baptist churches, one in Brownsville and the other in Eugene.[53]

As a result of the gold rush, Oregon established an efficient trade system, more new settlers came into the Pacific Northwest, and pioneers such as Abernethy, Nesmith, Spores, and Smith profited from their various business enterprises. But what about the Oregon adventurers who went to California to try their luck in the mining districts? Although some prospectors were unlucky, returning with little more than when they left, strong evidence indicates that many Oregonians were successful in California. The "Columbia River men," as they were called, fared well because they were among the first to arrive at the goldfields and they remained together. When one of their number discovered a promising stream or lode, he would inform the rest, and within a short time, Oregonians would be prospecting elbow to elbow. In 1848 a large number of northwesterners congregated on the Yuba and Feather rivers;[54] then in 1849 many of these same miners along with newcomers moved to the American River and founded Hangtown (later Placerville).[55]

Oregonians usually returned to their farms in the Willamette Valley after their experiences in the goldfields. Some remained in California for two or three years, or until they became convinced that their efforts were no longer profitable. Others returned to their farms for several months and then made additional trips south to work their claims. There were also the unfortunate ones who had not yet recouped their expenses from the overland trip and simply could not afford to go to the mines. P. W. Crawford was so eager that he worked at thirteen different jobs — everything from surveying to hauling barrel staves for salmon canning — to earn enough money for equipment and provisions to join his fellow Oregonians in California.[56]

The *Oregon City Oregon Spectator* provided an early source of information on the success of Oregonians. In February 1849 the newspaper reported that passengers on board the *Malek Adhel* brought $120,000 in gold dust from the mining districts.[57] Prospectors also wrote to their relatives and friends back home telling of their general welfare and success in the goldfields. One such letter was written by Donald McLeod to Alvin T. Smith on 4 July 1849. After several months of searching for a good claim, McLeod said, he "at last spread [his] tent on a Revere [*sic*] that empties in the Macolamey [Mokelumne] River and remained with tolerable good success until the 25th of June for which I dug out $3746." The miner also informed his friend that he "delivered to Captain Crosby for safe keeping $3000 in dust [and] a purse containing 11 ounces of large gold — the heaviest pes [piece] $40."[58]

Years later, some of the more fortunate adventurers penned their stories for posterity. In 1900 H. S. Lyman told the story of a Mr. Hudson who left his farm in the Willamette Valley near Oregon City, went to the mining districts, and found a pocket of ore that yielded over $22,000 in gold. Hudson was probably a little bit more eccentric than his fellow prospectors. He paid an ounce in gold dust each day to have his meals prepared and brought to him. Lyman also wrote about his friend Hugh Cosgrove who was in California in 1848 and 1849. On his first trip, Cosgrove stayed for one month; his second journey lasted twenty months. When Cosgrove returned, he brought back over $20,000 from his prospecting and the earnings received from selling a store in the Mother Lode.[59] James Duval Holman followed the crowds south in 1848 and found his fortune on the Feather and American rivers. While Holman was in California, John Sutter offered him the position of administrator over all his holdings in the Sacramento Valley. Holman turned down the job — the same one Peter Burnett later accepted. Upon returning to Oregon City, Holman invested in a ferry and store. He later sold his business interests and moved to Washington Territory.[60]

Forty years after the discovery of gold, the *Portland Oregonian* published a lengthy article recounting the history of the state. In the opinion of the editors, the gold rush marked the transformation of Oregon from a pioneer settlement to a vital participant in the modern age.

> Presto! Change! The pioneer days are gone. There is henceforth the rustle of the world, the dull glitter of gold, trade and commerce and all the thousand acts and things that identify man with civilization and a land with the great round world. . . . Henceforth the Oregonian is an active, integral part of the golden age.[61]

By 1850 the effects of the gold rush were beginning to wear off, and leading up to statehood in 1859, Oregon embarked on a period of sustained growth. Also in 1850, the federal government conducted its first census in the territory. Census takers enumerated the population by households, giving names, ages, and places of birth, as well as occupations of the adult males. They also had the option of filling in the spaces for the "value of real estate owned." Joseph Meek, who surveyed Clackamas County, attempted to list land values, but in certain cases, especially agricultural land, he tended to exaggerate the value of real property. For example, although Lot Whitcomb, the founder of Milwaukie, Oregon, was a wealthy man, his holdings in that town probably were not worth the $200,000 Meek indicated.[62] On the other hand, Meek's assessments of houses in Oregon City were nearly identical to other available real estate figures from the same period. The commonly cited cost of $17,000 for Dr. Forbes Barclay's house, therefore, is confirmed by the census, which declared the value (house and land) at $20,000.[63]

OREGON'S CARPENTERS

As manuscript data, the census yields its greatest value as a source for analyzing patterns in the Oregon populace. For instance, the owners of classical houses made up only a small percentage of the Oregon population. This study has identified thirty-two Greek Revival residences in Oregon, and of that number, reliable documentation has survived for twenty-six owners.[64] Biographies and census data indicate that twenty-three (88 percent) lived in the Midwest for various lengths of time before coming to Oregon.[65] While these figures do not give conclusive evidence that Oregon pioneers copied midwestern architectural styles, they certainly suggest that many, if not all, of these people had seen midwestern Greek Revival houses before they came to the Far West.

In other ways, the 1850 census demonstrates a strong midwestern influence in the Oregon population. As indicated earlier, Jesse Douglas concluded that pioneers from the Atlantic states played more important roles in the development of Oregon than previously realized; but he also demonstrated that the Midwest provided an even greater influence as the "crucible in which the population of the Pacific Northwest was molded."[66]

Douglas's findings have been confirmed by the later research of Dorothy O. Johansen. She investigated 1,300 land claim applications

113

before 1851 and discovered that 66 percent of the applicants were married in Ohio, Indiana, Illinois, or Missouri.[67] More recently, William Bowen has presented the most comprehensive study of the 1850 census in his book *Willamette Valley: Migration and Settlement on the Oregon Frontier* (1978). Like Douglas and Johansen, he concludes that a majority of Oregonians came from the Midwest and presents an impressive series of maps to substantiate his contention. These maps illustrate the origins and migration patterns and pinpoint where groups of Willamette Valley residents were living in 1850. For example, he shows that most New Englanders settled in towns such as Oregon City and Portland, while a large majority of midwesterners lived in rural areas.[68]

Clearly, Greek Revival house owners shared common traits with fellow Oregonians. Most came from the Midwest. Many were not skilled carpenters and had to hire local craftsmen to build their residences. It would have been most convenient if these house owners had kept records indicating who did their building for them. Perhaps they did, but the records simply did not survive. Fortunately, though, the population records provide a useful indication of the number and origins of the carpenters in Oregon in 1850.

The census lists 194 carpenters or building-related tradesmen, about 6 percent of the adult male population.[69] Of these individuals, forty-six were single young men living in Oregon City or Portland.[70] They did not own any property in 1850 and were not included in the census as builders ten years later. Perhaps these men were members of building crews during the gold rush who worked different jobs when the economy stabilized after 1851. The remaining 148 carpenters lived in various locations throughout the territory. Most owned real property, were married, and supported their families with the income derived from their trade. Unlike single men, 57 percent of these individuals remained in the same trade in 1860. Besides the identified craftsmen, an undetermined number of skilled carpenters probably were omitted from the census. In other words, while many men were listed as farmers, they were just as capable of constructing ornamented houses. Alvin T. Smith, William Case, and John Phillips fit into this category and demonstrated their carpentry skills by building their own Greek Revival houses.[71] It is significant, however, that 148 carpenters derived adequate income from their work in 1850, and that many remained in the same profession ten years later.

As for the origins of these craftsmen, 72 percent, or 106, lived in the Midwest before coming to Oregon.[72] Seventy-five lived in the middle states for at least ten years. In all likelihood, most observed examples of Greek Revival architecture in the Midwest, and many had probably worked on such buildings. The remaining thirty-one came from eastern and southern states or foreign countries and resided in the Midwest for less than ten years or for an undetermined period of time.[73] These figures closely correspond to the calculations of Douglas, Johansen, and Bowen for the general Oregon population and indicate that the backgrounds of these individuals were similar to other Oregonians.[74]

Many carpenters lived in more than one midwestern state before they came west. Yet the comparative numbers of builders from individual midwestern states were different. Missouri represented the largest group of pioneers in Oregon in 1850. But Ohio contributed more carpenters, with thirty-two, followed by Illinois and Missouri with sixteen apiece, Indiana and Iowa with six and four respectively, and Michigan with one. Forty-three of these craftsmen lived in rural areas of Oregon, and thirty-two lived in or near Oregon City and Portland.

Seventy-three emigrated from eastern and southern states or foreign countries. According to census records, forty-two were not from the Midwest, and thirty-one resided there for less than ten years or for inconclusive amounts of time. Of the seventy-three carpenters, forty-four came from New England, Pennsylvania, or New York; nineteen moved from southern states; and ten migrated from foreign countries. Sixty craftsmen from these groups lived in or near Oregon City and Portland, and thirteen resided in rural areas.[75]

In summary, at least 148 carpenters are known to have lived in Oregon in 1850. Of this number, 106 had resided in the Midwest, and seventy-five of these builders were residents there for at least ten years. Since many Greek Revival houses in Oregon resembled midwestern examples, it is likely that these carpenters had observed and some had built classical structures before coming to Oregon. That ninety-two builders were living in Portland and Oregon City indicates the rapid development of these towns during the gold rush. But the fact that fifty-eight builders settled outside of these communities suggests adequate opportunites in rural areas as well.

Rural carpenters built most of the Greek Revival houses in Oregon. Following the gold rush, sawn lumber was readily available from mills constructed to supply the mining districts. Builders brought with them or later acquired the necessary tools and equipment to execute the moldings and other features of classical architecture. The classical detailing work on most residences indicates that builders owned copies of pattern books or were familiar with the information these sources provided on Greek Revival details. After the bonanza period in Oregon, the increased wealth and the desire of some settlers to have a fancy new house gave carpenters the opportunity to practice their skills.

At the end of 1850, Alvin T. Smith recorded in his diary: "Cut and halled some wood. Thus close up another year of my pilgrimage here on earth." This year was productive for Smith. In addition to acquiring land in Hillsboro and purchasing a share in the steamship *Gold Hunter*, he started construction on the first building for Tualatin Academy, which later would become Pacific University. He also made a substantial profit by selling produce and livestock.[76] The year 1850 was beneficial for other Oregonians as well. It capped a decade in which the population had grown to about 12,000 people, the gold rush had boosted the economy, and Oregon had become a territory. Prosperity would continue for Smith and others into the next decade, and some would have enough money to build their Greek Revival houses.

5

Greek Revival Architecture in Oregon

Oregon's Greek Revival houses offer a great variety of architectural expression. From the elegant Captain John Ainsworth House in Oregon City to the plain Alvin T. Smith residence near Forest Grove, these houses are the result of different historical circumstances and display varying sizes, shapes, and detailing. For example, while the Ainsworth house was an architectural gem, almost no information survives concerning the designer, builder, or the construction techniques. On the other hand, although Smith's dwelling was not as aesthetically pleasing, the owner recorded a wealth of data about the construction process in his diary. Together, the Ainsworth, Smith, and other Greek Revival structures built in Oregon during the 1850s offer an excellent opportunity to understand cultural history through the built environment.

ALVIN T. SMITH HOUSE

Alvin T. Smith's daily journal provides a bridge between the 1840s and the 1850s in Oregon. Following the gold rush, he continued to operate his farm, lend money to his neighbors, and serve as a church leader. Smith's diary indicates that he prospered from his investments between 1848 and 1850. By 1851, however, he returned to his pre–gold rush activities. In 1853 he diversified his agricultural interests by planting twenty fruit saplings purchased from Seth Lewelling, the pioneer horticulturalist in the Northwest. A year later, he began building his new house.[1]

Though Smith had amassed enough wealth to hire a carpenter, he chose to design and construct his Greek Revival house himself. He had sharpened his carpentry skills three years earlier while helping build the Tualatin Academy with several church associates.[2] When he completed that major project, he decided to erect a fancy new house. In characteristic fashion Smith's diary leaves the reader wanting more information — such as why he selected the Greek Revival style — but it is not difficult to forgive him for these omissions. His descriptions, although brief, give the only account of the construction process for an 1850s Oregon house. He built the residence in about eighteen months, accomplishing most of the work without outside help.[3]

From June through September 1854, Smith simply recorded that he worked on "the new house." In October he shingled the second story, and a month later he attached a lean-to on the side of the main structure.[4] During 1855 the house continued to take shape. He purchased glass in Portland in September, finished laying the floor in November, and agreed to pay E. D. Whitlow $15.73 for crafting a fireplace mantle and fixing roof leaks in December. Except for repairs and minor finishing work, the house was completed by New Year's Day 1856 (Figure 1.1). During the construction phase, Smith periodically bought lumber from a local mill, making his final purchase in November 1855.

Smith's diary provides specific and inferential information about the construction of the new house. Whitlow probably was a local cabinetmaker specializing in decorative features, such as doors, sashes, and other house furnishings. Perhaps he owned a cabinet shop or simply was a carpenter with the proper tools and expertise to fashion moldings. In either case, Smith's reference to him demonstrates that a craftsman was available nearby in 1855.[5] Smith's journey to Portland to purchase glass suggests that this commodity was not yet locally available. Milled lumber and shingles, however, could be purchased only a short distance from the building site.[6]

Smith's house survives today as an unusual example of Greek Revival architecture in Oregon. Few northwest builders chose the temple form plan for their houses. Smith selected this building plan because it reminded him of houses in his hometown in Connecticut. Whether he recalled the plan and detailing from memory or developed the design from a pattern book is not known. Builders generally did not make exact copies of house elevations from pattern books, so even if Smith used one of these sources, it is not surprising that an exact plan is not readily discernible. Smith designed a floor plan that met his needs. The lean-to attached to the side of the house appears to be a later addition; his diary, however, clearly indicates that this feature was, for reasons known only to him, included in the original plan.[7] As another innovation for Oregon, Smith placed his house on a solid brick foundation rather than on the typical brick or stone pier base.

The classical detailing included an unusually broad entablature with simple cyma recta moldings and bold eave returns at the gable ends suggesting a pediment. Delicate pilasters with simple caps supported and decorated the corners. While the engaged columns were functional, they were much smaller than the entablature and thus appeared inadequate to hold this massive feature. Again, Smith was more concerned with creating a house that met his needs rather than with building a work of art. The fact that the scale of the entablature and pilasters might look awkward to twentieth-century critics was of little concern to him.[8]

WILLIAM CASE HOUSE

Other Oregonians built large, elaborate residences comparable to the finest dwellings in the Midwest, South, or East. Such an example is the William Case House in Champoeg. Case and his wife, Sarah, left northern Missouri and traveled overland to Oregon in 1844. William was born in Virginia or Louisiana and his wife came from New Jersey.[9] They met and were married in Indiana and had intended to migrate to Oregon in 1841. They arrived at the rendezvous point on the Missouri River after the wagon trains had departed and decided to remain in Missouri until the next spring. During the year, Case worked as a carpenter and mechanic, and thus the one-year stopover stretched to three. The Cases finally arrived in Oregon in 1844, and William went to work building barns in the Tualatin Valley near present-day Hillsboro. In 1846 they settled three miles from the Willamette River near Champoeg. Case built a comfortable four-room log cabin, started cultivating the land, and constructed barns and houses for his neighbors. He probably would have been content to stay on the farm for the rest of his life except that he, like many of his fellow Oregonians, caught "gold fever" in 1848.

Case traveled to San Francisco on board the bark *Anita* and went directly to the mines. He quickly observed that he could "mine" the miners with his carpentry skills. By erecting buildings and operating a store, he cleared about $2,800 in seven months. Returning to the Willamette Valley with this newly acquired capital, Case purchased equipment and built a sawmill on his land claim. With the profits from his lumber business, he expanded his operation by constructing a tile and brick factory and an iron smelter. All of Case's enterprises were successful. He eventually acquired 1,500 acres of land, and when he died in 1903 at the age of eighty-three, he was a very wealthy man.[10]

Four years after Case returned from the gold rush, he began building a new house. The project took seven years, partly because Case kept selling the necessary lumber and bricks to his neighbors. Also, the residence was so huge it required a great deal of time and money to finish. When completed, the house measured 150 by 70 feet — substantial dimensions considering that the attached woodshed portion (thirty-eight feet square) was larger than many Oregon pioneer residences (Figures 5.1–5.4). Size was only one unique feature. The woodshed contained a well seventy-two feet deep and a firebox to heat water for bathing and laundry. Significantly, all the materials — bricks, nails, and lumber — were manufactured on site.[12]

In terms of style, the Case House is unlike any other in the Pacific Northwest. Case was born in either Virginia or Louisiana — the record is unclear — and lived in Indiana and Missouri before coming to Oregon. Thus his house should have been similar to those in one of these states. Here the plot thickens. Case's residence and the Narcisse Prudhomme Plantation House in Louisiana were similar in style, massing, detailing, and dimensions (Figure 5.5). If Case came from Louisiana, or more precisely Natchitoches Parish, there would be an obvious connection between the two structures. On the other hand, if he came from Virginia and had never visited Louisiana, the resemblance is harder to explain.[12]

Even though Case's residence was one of the largest in Oregon, it was not visible from the main road only a few hundred feet away. Seclusion was not the criterion for the building site. Case recognized that the location afforded protection from winter weather, offered a view of trees and an expansive valley, and provided close proximity to a water supply as well as all of his business enterprises. To take advantage of the setting, Case featured a continuous gallery supported by thirty-one turned wooden pillars surrounding the entire structure and presenting the most dramatic representation of classical architecture in Oregon. Yet the column capitals presented an anomaly typical of many Oregon Greek Revival houses. Similar to the Roman Tuscan and the Greek Doric orders, but not distinguishable as either, Case presented his interpretation of classical design. His creative touch blended well with the rest of the structure and its surroundings.

The historical record does not indicate whether Case owned an architectural pattern book. The evidence of the gallery columns, however,

Figure 5.1: William Case House, Champoeg, Oregon. Built by William Case, 1860. *Courtesy Oregon State Parks.*

Figure 5.2: William Case House, Champoeg, Oregon. Built by William Case, 1860. *Courtesy Oregon State Parks.*

Figure 5.3: William Case House, Champoeg, Oregon. Built by William Case, 1860. *Courtesy Oregon State Parks.*

Figure 5.4: William Case House, Champoeg, Oregon. Built by William Case, 1860. *Courtesy Oregon State Parks.*

suggests that he was familiar with the information from these sources. He borrowed the technique of entasis from the Parthenon. By crafting a slight convex curve into each column, he gave them a sprightly appearance, suggesting that they could carry substantial weight. Case apparently decided that the open gallery was sufficient to give his house a classical appearance. Molded eave cornices above the columns and a pediment created by the meeting of the gable roof and the gallery cornice were the only other Greek Revival features on the exterior.

On the interior, Case did not spare expense or effort to make the space beautiful and comfortable. He and his wife raised thirteen children, and the house included six bedrooms to accommodate the large family. John Shatz, a local craftsman, built the cabinets and the mantles and finished much of the interior. He skillfully joined the horizontal interior boards, giving the walls an appearance of a plaster finish. The living quarters were located on the first floor, and the half-story attic, which ran the entire length of the house, was never finished. Case family relics, such as an old copper bathtub, are stored here, and the walls are covered with newspaper — a nineteenth-century insulation technique.[13]

Figure 5.5: Narcisse Prudhomme Plantation House, Natchitoches vicinity, Louisiana, ca. 1800. *Courtesy John C. Guillet.*

CAPTAIN JOHN C. AINSWORTH HOUSE

Most Oregonians who built classical houses either were farmers or, like Case, included farming as one of several vocations. One notable exception, however, was Captain John C. Ainsworth. Born in Ohio in 1822, Ainsworth lived in the Ohio and upper Mississippi valleys before he came West. He was a skilled river captain and owner of a small steamboat on the Mississippi. He went to California in 1850, and although he made a salary of $20,000 per year as an assistant court clerk, he was so disgusted with the lawlessness there, he stayed on for only three months. He then went to work for two Oregon entrepreneurs piloting the newly completed steamship *Lot Whitcomb*. In a short time, he became a legendary figure for his prowess as a Pacific Northwest riverboat captain. Among his most memorable feats, Ainsworth surpassed earlier speed records between Astoria and Portland by making the trip in ten hours; he negotiated the narrow Willamette River channel between Milwaukie and Oregon City in less than one hour; and he piloted the steamboat that defeated the *Willamette* in a much-heralded race on the Columbia River between Portland and St. Helens in 1851.[14]

By 1856, as owner of the *Belle*, Ainsworth piloted the vessel on regular trips on the Columbia River above Portland. Then, in 1860, he created one of the most successful and powerful businesses in the Pacific Northwest — the Oregon Steam Navigation Company. His firm was a partnership between prominent Oregon businessmen and owners of the portages on the Oregon and Washington sides at the Cascade Rapids of the Columbia. Ainsworth became the president of the corporation and held that position for eighteen of the nineteen years the company was in existence. The Oregon Steam Navigation Company began service to the interior Northwest at about the same time gold was discovered in Idaho and Montana. Steamboats provided regular service from Portland to Lewiston, Idaho, by way of the Columbia and Snake rivers, and into British Columbia on the upper Columbia. Eventually vessels ran on Lake Pend d'Oreille, up the Clark's Fork to within 125 miles of Fort Benton and the Missouri River, and on the upper Snake River. But by the late 1870s, railroads were making their way into the Oregon country, and the company was sold to Henry Villard for $5,000,000.[15] Following the sale, Ainsworth invested in real estate in Washington Territory, built the Ainsworth Block commercial building in Portland, and in 1883 became a banker. He eventually extended his business activities to Oakland, California, where he died in 1893.[16]

Captain Ainsworth is usually remembered for his business activities in the Pacific Northwest, but his house near Oregon City is an important legacy for the architectural historian. Unfortunately, little documentation has survived about the structure. Recently, an Ainsworth descendant donated the Captain's handwritten autobiography to the Oregon Historical Society. Perhaps, at long last, all questions about the house would be answered. For example, who built his house? How much did it cost? Why did he select the unique design? Such was not the case. In fact, Ainsworth said in his autobiography that this house was one of his rare investment disasters. He poured thousands into the property, then traded it for mining stocks that proved worthless. Thus, what would have been a dream house to most Oregonians turned out to be a nightmare for Captain Ainsworth.[17]

Fortunately, questions not answered in manuscripts can be solved circumstantially. Ainsworth was not a carpenter and was busy piloting the *Lot Whitcomb* while the house was under construction in the early 1850s. Thus he hired a carpenter or a crew of craftsmen for the project. Clues suggest a possible name for the builder and his origins. The massing, classical detailing, and configuration of the Ainsworth residence bear a striking resemblance to the Aull House in Lexington, Missouri (Figure 3.21). Ainsworth may have seen this dwelling, or more likely, the carpenter was familiar with this or other such structures in Missouri. The Oregon census lists four carpenters from Missouri living in Oregon City in 1850. Of these craftsmen, Nathaniel Hamlin and Milton Brown had resided in Missouri for at least five years each, and both owned real property valued at $3,000 and $4,000 respectively in Oregon City. The execution of detailing on the residence required skill and expensive equipment. Since these two men were the only carpenters there who owned property, they probably possessed the high-priced tools needed for the job.[18]

Whether Hamlin or Brown built the house is an interesting question; however, the house he created is an architectural masterpiece (Figure 3.22). The combination of the dramatic front portico, the sophisticated craftsmanship throughout, and the setting on a prominent hill south of Oregon City makes this structure one of the most elaborate — of any style — in Oregon. The designer must have built Greek Revival houses before he came west, because his execution of classical details demonstrated a skill not seen on most 1850s Oregon houses. The front portico provided a focal point for the Greek Revival format. Four octagonal, tapered pillars appear as solid marble or timber, but actually each is hollow, constructed with eight strips of lumber with attached laths to give a fluted appearance. The column capitals were more complex than the Greek Doric order and somewhat of a cross between Tuscan and Roman Doric. On the corners of the front facade, the column motif was duplicated on the two flat pilasters. A balcony on the second story, which was recessed and separate from the pillars, provided an effective break in the plain appearance of the front facade. Because of the narrow dimensions created by the temple front, the designer opted for the side-hall plan to provide more space in the parlor and the upstairs bedrooms. Large front windows and the side and transom windows flanking the main entryway offered interior brightness during the gloomy Oregon winters. A full Tuscan entablature with a center molding strip to divide the architrave and the frieze surrounded the main block. It continued on the pediment and the eave returns on the back of the structure. The same entablature motif was scaled down in size and placed over the front windows and doorway as pedimented cornices.

On the interior, the Ainsworth House has remained essentially unchanged. The carefully planned dimensions and detailing of the temple plan on the exterior, however, created cramped living quarters and led an owner in the late 1800s to add a two-story bay on the east facade to allow more light and room.[19] The interior plan included a parlor, living and dining rooms on the first floor, and bedrooms upstairs. A large second-floor ballroom in the ell extension was an unusual feature for an Oregon house, suggesting that Ainsworth enjoyed entertaining.[20]

HUGH FIELDS HOUSE

About a hundred miles south of the Ainsworth House, the Hugh Fields House near Brownsville stands as the other surviving example of a tetrastyle (four-columned) temple format residence in Oregon (Figure 5.6). The jigsawn classical motifs of the full entablature, in addition to the four stylized columns, offer a stunning presentation of Greek Revival architecture on the front portico and pediment. Particularly noteworthy is the molding panel placed on the upper edge of the frieze of the front entablature and over the windows and doors. Here, the craftsman cut a continuous semicircular design that is unprecedented in Oregon or elsewhere. The columns and pilasters, as well, were topped with interesting capitals that also defy comparison with other examples. Like the designer of the Ainsworth House, the builder created beauty without following prescribed classical design guidelines.

Fields arrived in Oregon in 1845 as a young lad of seventeen years. He spent his first year assisting Sam Barlow in building the Barlow Road from The Dalles around the south side of Mt. Hood. During the next couple of years, he helped immigrants pull their wagons over this same route. Then, in 1848, he could not resist the pull of the California mines. He prospected near Hangtown (Placerville) for nearly a year and returned with a reported $4,000 in gold dust. Following his California adventure, Fields returned to Oregon and settled in Brownsville where he eventually acquired about 1,000 acres, including the land on which this house was located. He remained in Brownsville until 1870, and during that time he engaged in a number of profitable enterprises, built his house in about 1859, then rented his farm and went to eastern

127

Figure 5.6: Hugh Fields House, Brownsville, Oregon. Unknown designer, ca. 1859. *Courtesy Marion Dean Ross*.

Oregon where he became the baron of a 6,000-acre cattle and sheep ranch. This venture, in addition to his other investments, eventually left Fields overextended. When he died in 1901, his estate could not cover his debts. Although Fields's business legacy has long since been forgotten, his house remains a unique interpretation of Oregon Greek Revival architecture.[21]

SAM BROWN HOUSE

One year after Hugh Fields's arrival, Sam and Elizabeth Brown started for Oregon with the intention of settling in the Willamette Valley. At Fort Hall, however, employees of the Hudson's Bay Company persuaded them to alter their course and head for California. They settled on the Feather River where Sam constructed and operated a sawmill for a time. With the discovery of gold, all the workers left, so the Browns decided to try their luck in the nearby placers. Within a year the Brown claim yielded about $20,000 in gold. The couple soon left for Oregon, arriving in the Willamette Valley in 1850 and settling on a farm near Gervais. During the first six years there, the couple lived in a log cabin, but in 1856 they started building a new house. It was completed in 1858 at a cost of about $10,000.[22]

Family tradition holds that the Brown House was designed by a local builder, another Sam Brown, who was no relation.[23] Whether this Brown built the residence is of little consequence, because the dwelling itself is more significant than the name of its designer (Figure 5.7). In appearance the Brown House is the only extant example in Oregon of a Greek temple with flanking wings. A number of similar houses exist throughout the country, including two noteworthy prototypes in the eastern United States. Although not Greek Revival in style, Thomas Jefferson's plan for his first Monticello (Figure 5.8), before it was remodeled, was similar in appearance to the Brown House. Federal Hill in Campbell County, Virginia (Figure 5.9), was also nearly identical to the early Monticello in style and building plan. Federal Hill was the home of James Steptoe, a Jefferson classmate at William and Mary College and a lifelong friend. Further, it was probably inspired, if not designed, by Jefferson. In addition to these two examples, Minard Lafever included a plan for a similar country villa with a central block and two flanking wings in plate 322 of his *The Beauties of Modern Architecture* (1833) (Figure 5.10). Although neither Brown nor his carpenter probably saw the two Virginia houses, they perhaps studied Lafever's model.[24]

129

Figure 5.7: Sam Brown House, Gervais, Oregon. Built by Sam Brown, 1856. *Courtesy Oregon State Parks.*

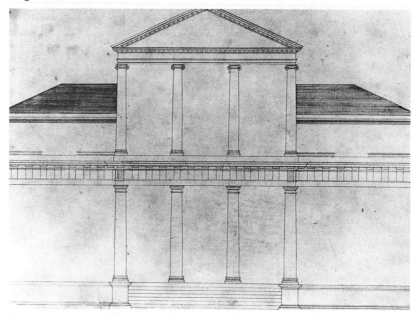

Figure 5.8: Monticello (first design), Charlottesville, Virginia. Designed by Thomas Jefferson, ca. 1775. *Courtesy Thomas Jefferson Memorial Foundation.*

Figure 5.9: Federal Hill (James Steptoe House), Campbell County, Virginia. Unknown designer, ca. 1800. *Courtesy Virginia Department of Historic Resources.*

The Brown House featured a two-story front portico as the principal representation of the Greek vocabulary. A simple entablature surrounded the main block or temple section, creating a full pediment. Inside the portico, a second-story porch with lattice railing was a delicate addition that provided a shady veranda for warm weather. According to an 1860s photograph, the two square columns on the portico were "marbleized" or textured with paint to appear like stone pillars (Figure 5.11).[25]

During the 1860s and early 1870s the Brown House was a stopping point on the main stage line between Portland and Eugene. As a result, many of the rooms in the house became sleeping quarters for passengers during the winter. The story-and-a-half wings contained bedrooms upstairs and downstairs, and the upper level of the central block section also was a dormitory. Behind the main structure, two separate wings included a boys room on the north and a kitchen, pantry, and fruit storeroom on the south. The main house and wings were connected by covered passageways, and the three structures surrounded an open courtyard.[26]

The Brown House survives essentially intact due, in part, to excellent construction techniques. Hand-hewn timbers, braced together

131

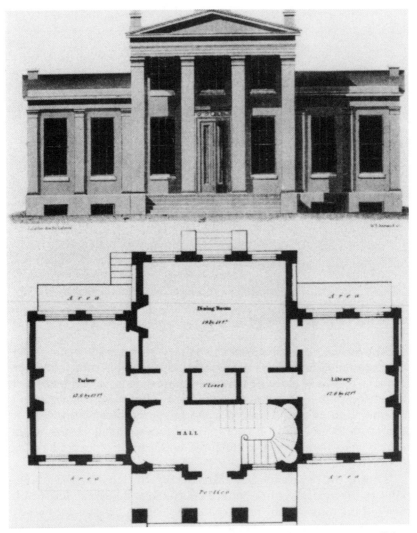

Figure 5.10: Country villa elevation with a central block with two flanking wings. Taken from Minard Lafever, *The Beauties of Modern Architecture*, 1833.

Figure 5.11: Sam Brown House, Gervais, Oregon. Built by Sam Brown, 1856. *Courtesy Oregon State Parks.*

and connected with wooden pegs, make up the framing system.[27] The hand-split and -shaved cedar shingles, which lasted for over eighty years, received an award for durability at the 1940 Oregon State Fair. Eave gutters were fashioned from fifty-foot-long cedar trees and covered with sheet metal. The craftsmanship of the Brown House is superior, and the condition, the plan, the detailing, and even the original furnishings have remained intact, because the Brown family has lived in and cared for the dwelling since its completion.

Sam Brown operated a 1,500-acre farm and stagecoach station with the house as his headquarters. He also started a family political tradition, serving as a state senator from 1866 to 1872. His son, Sam Brown II, followed in his father's footsteps by residing in the house, serving as state representative from 1915 to 1918 and state senator from 1923 to 1934, and running unsuccessfully as the Republican candidate for governor in 1934. Sam Brown III presently lives in the house, the original furnishings remaining in their same locations.[28]

As a part of its rich heritage, a number of stories have survived concerning the Brown House. When it was the headquarters for farming activities and a stage station, several hired hands were employed on a full-time basis. One man was responsible for cutting and splitting forty cords of wood and keeping the four fireplaces and kitchen stove supplied during the winter. Hong, the Chinese cook, and two hired girls were in charge of preparing and serving meals to stage passengers and the hired hands. The first floor room in the northern wing of the main house was always kept available for circuit-riding ministers traveling throughout the Willamette Valley.[29]

JAMES BYBEE HOUSE

Sam Brown, William Case, Hugh Fields, and most of the early pioneers established their farms in the rich bottomlands of the Willamette Valley. Throughout the Pacific Northwest, however, there were other fertile farmlands. Sauvie Island, located at the confluence of the Willamette and Columbia rivers, was as rich in flora and fauna as any part of the territory. Recent archeological excavations as well as the reports of early explorers reveal a substantial Indian culture. The Hudson's Bay Company used the pasturage for a dairy herd, and Nathaniel Wyeth located a temporary trading station, Fort William, on the island in 1834. Although Sauvie Island was a desirable area to settle, its small size precluded many farmers from establishing claims. James Bybee, his wife, Julia, and their two small children were among the few families who established farms on the island.

Available biographical information indicates that the Bybees came to Oregon from Kentucky in 1847 and settled on their farm in 1848. The same source states that later that year James went alone to the California mines. The Bybees, however, were not listed in the 1850 census and such conflicting information suggests several possibilities. Perhaps the family settled in Oregon at a later date; or maybe Julia Bybee and her children accompanied James to the mines. Yet another more likely explanation was that the census taker simply did not include Sauvie Island in his survey. In any event, little is known about James Bybee in California, except that an unnamed contemporary source stated that he "made a fortune." When he returned to Oregon in about 1850, he settled on his farm on Sauvie Island.[30]

While James was in California, his cousin William Bybee also arrived in the goldfields. Apparently the two men made contact there, because William headed north to visit his cousin on Sauvie Island in about 1851. He stayed for a year, then moved to Jacksonville in southern Oregon and bought a farm. Dorothy Johansen found that family members often followed their relatives to Oregon, so William Bybee's visit to his cousin was not uncommon.[31] What was unusual was that

Figure 5.12: James Bybee House, Sauvie Island, Oregon. Unknown builder, 1856. *Courtesy Oregon State Parks.*

both men eventually built houses that were remarkably similar in size and appearance.[32]

James Bybee's residence, sited on the highest point of Sauvie Island, is a two-story frame structure with a kitchen ell attached to the rear (Figure 5.12). The Greek detailing was restrained, yet carefully executed. A full Tuscan entablature surrounded the structure at the eaves, creating two full pediments on the side gable ends. The head moldings over the windows and doorways represented modified forms of the Tuscan entablature. Two square columns, capped with Tuscan capitals, supported the front porch, and the same motif was carried over to the corner and portico pilasters. Inside, the residence displayed some of the finest finishing techniques of any early house in Oregon. The walls, cornices, and ceilings were plastered, and the ceilings in the dining room and parlor were decorated with elaborate sculptured plaster chandelier medallions.[33] The oak floors in the hallway and most of the house, the redwood-paneled library, the built-in sideboard in the dining room, and the white maple floors, doors, and molding in the parlor created an elegant interior. Seven fireplaces, each with slightly varied classical detailing, continued the Greek Revival theme within the house.[34]

As it turned out, James Bybee contracted a more serious case of "gold fever" than many of his fellow Oregonians. In 1858, two years after building his new house, he sold his Donation Land Claim to Dr. Benjamin Howell and went to British Columbia to seek another fortune. Howell came to Oregon in 1850 from New Jersey, and he and his descendants lived in the house and farmed the land for more than a century. Multnomah County acquired the Bybee-Howell House and a portion of the farm in 1961 and gave the Oregon Historical Society the responsibility of preserving and maintaining the dwelling. The house was badly deteriorated and covered with vegetation, but volunteer and professional crews systematically restored it, collected period furniture for the interior, cleared the underbrush, and carefully pruned the historical fruit trees.[35] As a result, the Bybee-Howell House is now open to the public and is an Oregon showcase for Greek Revival architecture.

WILLIAM BYBEE HOUSE

While James Bybee stayed on his land for only a short time, William Bybee remained in Jacksonville until his death in 1908. For forty years, his principal occupation was buying and driving hogs to mining and logging camps in northern California and southern Oregon. In 1878 and 1880 he was elected sheriff of Jackson County, and by about 1890 he was one of the major landholders in the Rogue River Valley. At his death, the local newspaper eulogized him as one of the most prominent citizens in southern Oregon.[36]

William Bybee's house especially resembles his cousin's residence on the front facade, displaying similar fenestration and an identical porch (Figure 5.13). The main body of the structure was narrower, but the larger ell extension on the rear provided nearly an equal amount of living space. Tuscan order capitals on the porch columns, pilasters, and entablature were nearly interchangeable with the Sauvie Island house. Eave returns instead of a full pediment were a major difference in this house, which also detracted somewhat from its appearance. Inside, William Bybee's house displayed the same careful craftsmanship as its "cousin," with similar artistic attention paid to the plaster detailing. Concentric circles of plaster on the ceiling surrounded an elaborate molded chandelier medallion. The pine doors were grained with varnish to give the wood a more expensive appearance. Fireplaces in the parlor and three other rooms were decorated with classical mantles.[37] Together, the interiors of the two Bybee houses

Figure 5.13: William Bybee House, Jacksonville, Oregon. Unknown designer, 1858. *Courtesy Oregon State Parks.*

demonstrated an uncommon artistic sophistication when compared with other Oregon dwellings of the same period.

JACOB SPORES HOUSE

In many ways, William and James Bybee were typical of Oregon pioneers. Both were young (twenty-three and thirty, respectively) when they arrived in the Pacific Northwest, one being a bachelor and the other having a small family. In comparison, Jacob Spores, another classical house owner, was an atypical immigrant. In 1847, at the age of fifty-two, he and his second wife, Nancy, and most of his seventeen children made the overland trek to Oregon. Spores was born in Montgomery County, New York, and served in the War of 1812. In 1814 he and his first wife, Eliza, left New York to live in Ohio. After several years, the Spores moved again and purchased a farm near Springfield, Illinois, where Eliza died. Within a few years, Jacob married Nancy, who was seventeen years his junior, and the couple continued to live in Illinois for at least the next fourteen years.[38] When the Spores family left for Oregon in 1847, it probably dominated the wagon train, since several of the children had families of their own. When Jacob arrived

Figure 5.14: Jacob Spores House, Coburg, Oregon. Unknown builder, ca. 1854. *Courtesy Oregon State Parks.*

Figure 5.15: Jacob Spores House, Coburg, Oregon. Unknown builder, ca. 1854. *Courtesy Oregon State Parks.*

in Oregon, he established a farm near Eugene and a ferry across the McKenzie River. He made a substantial amount of money from both enterprises during the California gold rush, and using his newly acquired wealth, Spores built a Greek Revival house in about 1854.[39]

The close similarity in appearance between the Spores House (Figures 5.14–5.15) and the Newton Farmhouse in Illinois (Figure 3.19) suggests that perhaps Jacob or his carpenter was influenced by this or another midwestern classical structure when building the new house.[40] During a recent restoration, Gregg A. Olsen, the present owner, made a careful investigation of the construction technology and archeological materials and found definite similarities between the building details and site plans for both houses.

Also during the restoration, Olsen identified and replaced missing sections of the house, using historical tools and instructions from Asher Benjamin's books. The entablature, moldings, capitals, the foundation sill beams, and other features were fabricated with the methods employed by nineteenth-century builders. He found that the old tools were relatively easy to use and efficient for replicating classical details. For example, Olsen discovered that the carpenters had fashioned most of the classical moldings with two or three planes. A cyma reversa plane created an architrave base by shaving both edges of a cedar board. Planes commonly used for bullnosing or curving stair tread heads created pilaster capitals.[41] From an early lithographic print, as well as physical evidence, he duplicated the missing components of the original residence.

The Spores House was a double-plan structure with two large rooms in the main body of the structure, each with separate entrances and two identical bedrooms in the upstairs half-story. A one-level ell on the rear probably contained the kitchen and pantry. The front porch was a later addition that Olsen retained in the restoration project. To demonstrate that this feature was not historical, he left the columns uncapped. On the exterior, classical detailing on the entablature and corner pilasters were the house's most prominent features, and returns at the gable ends represented pediments.[42]

On the interior, nearly all original detailing was lost in a 1900 fire and in subsequent remodeling work. But Olsen uncovered evidence of the locations for historical features during the restoration. One of the walls was stripped of its paint and plaster, revealing the outline of a fireplace mantle. Although the discovery did not offer enough information to reconstruct the mantle, another fireplace panel with nearly identical dimensions became available some twenty miles away. The

Chatham Hawley House, built in 1855, was being demolished. Since its overall size, detailing, and date of construction were similar to the Spores House, Olsen decided to use its mantle for his fireplace (Figure 2.33). Not only did the borrowed feature enhance the interior of the Spores House, it also preserved an important artifact, for the panel is Oregon's only known example of a design taken from one of Asher Benjamin's handbooks.[43]

ANDREW SMITH HOUSE

As a whole, the restoration of the Spores House preserved an important cultural resource and provided important information on building techniques for an 1850s dwelling. Unfortunately, many vintage residences have been lost over the years, and others have been saved only at the eleventh hour. Such was the case with the Andrew Smith House in Dayton. In the spring of 1975, a concerned citizen called the Oregon State Historic Preservation Office to inform the staff that the Andrew Smith House was about to be burned by the local fire department for firefighting practice. The staff was not familiar with the structure, but the architect and historian went to Dayton to analyze the house and ascertain if it should be preserved. Upon their arrival, they discovered a remarkable structure that, despite its deterioration, contained nearly all of its original detailing. The staff members convinced the owners to save the dwelling and assisted them in placing it in the National Register of Historic Places.[44]

Upon investigation, the historian discovered that Andrew Smith was a little-known figure in Oregon history. According to the census and scanty biographical data, he was born in England and lived in Ohio before he immigrated to Oregon. He came across the plains in 1842 and settled in Yamhill County in 1844, where he operated a ferry on the Yamhill River. In 1848 he married the daughter of Joel Palmer, the Oregon superintendent of Indian affairs from 1853 to 1856. Smith and Palmer were partners in several business ventures, such as platting and subdividing the town of Dayton, Oregon, and prospecting in the Canadian Fraser River gold rush in 1859 and 1860.[45] While Smith was in British Columbia, he received a letter from his wife stating that this new residence was completed, and that there was a possible purchaser for the old one. The new structure undoubtedly was the Greek Revival house, which would place the date of construction at 1859.[46]

Figure 5.16: Andrew Smith House, Dayton, Oregon. Unknown designer, ca. 1859. *Courtesy Oregon State Parks.*

Figure 5.17: Andrew Smith House, Dayton, Oregon. Unknown designer, ca. 1859. *Courtesy Oregon State Parks.*

Architecturally, the Andrew Smith House resembles the Spores residence in size and detailing. Both structures are one-and-a-half stories high with the gable ends on the sides and kitchen ells attached to the rear (Figures 5.16–5.17). The Smith House differs from the Spores House in that it features a central hall rather than a double-house plan. Also in its presentation of classical detailing, Smith's home stands apart from the Spores's dwelling or any other comtemporary structure in Oregon. The builder chose the front facade as the focal point for the classical detailing. On this exposure, he created a bold cornice motif for the window and door caps and copied the same design on the pilaster capitals. Eave returns were omitted from the structure, which was unusual for an Oregon Greek Revival structure. In their place, a full entablature surrounded the entire house and pilasters with magnificent caps anchored each corner, including those on the kitchen ell.[49]

On the interior, the original floor plan has remained intact, and samples of the original wallpaper have survived under subsequent layers. Although a cedar post and beam structural system supported the dwelling, the state preservation staff noted in its 1975 inspection that the sill beam foundation on the northeast corner of the house was rotten. Although this portion was askew, there were no signs of strain on the framing system, suggesting that the house would be returned to its true shape if the corner support member was replaced.[48]

DARIUS B. CARTWRIGHT HOUSE

Saving the Andrew Smith House was a triumph for historic preservation in Oregon, but unfortunately, other efforts to rescue architectural landmarks have not met with the same success. The Darius B. Cartwright residence near Lorane was a notable casualty. This magnificent structure was abandoned, became badly deteriorated, and was burned in 1973. The Historic American Building Survey recorded the Cartwright house in 1933, and the Oregon Historic Preservation Office assembled a file on the building before it was destroyed. From these sources, it is possible to piece together the history and architectural significance of the Cartwright dwelling.[49]

Darius B. Cartwright was born in New York state in 1814 and was a cousin of the famous Methodist circuit-riding minister Peter Cartwright. He moved to Illinois in the 1830s where he married N. M. McAllister; then he, his wife, and his family went to California in 1849 to seek their fortune in the goldfields. Within two years they left California and

Figure 5.18: Darius B. Cartwright House, Lorane, Oregon. Built by Darius B. Cartwright, ca. 1852. *Courtesy Historic American Building Survey.*

purchased 530 acres of land and a cabin near Lorane. Cartwright probably started building his new house shortly after he arrived in Oregon, for his biographical information indicates that in 1852 he bought lumber from the Mulveny Mill ten miles away from the house site. The new dwelling was strategically located on the west-side territorial road through the Willamette Valley, and stagecoaches and freight wagons began to stop at the Cartwright property while the residence was still under construction.[50]

Cartwright built a huge house — by Oregon standards — to accommodate the business opportunities afforded by the stagecoach line. In the main structure and the ell extensions, twelve bedrooms with space for four or five double beds each could sleep upwards of a hundred guests per night. The living room was as large as many hotel lobbies, and the pantry and kitchen (with running water) were substantial enough to comfortably handle all guests. Horse barns and a tavern rounded out the property, providing further indication that the house was built to cater to the stagecoach traffic. The detailing and overall appearance resemble the Bybee houses (Figures 5.12–5.13). At each end grand pediments with full entablatures were supported with massive capped pilasters (Figures 5.18–5.19). There likely was a formal

Figure 5.19: Darius B. Cartwright House, Lorane, Oregon. Built by Darius B. Cartwright, ca. 1852. *Courtesy Oregon State Parks.*

porch supported by classical columns at the front entrance as well, although this feature was substantially altered when the house was recorded by the Historic American Building Survey in the 1930s.

In 1866 Cartwright sold the house and all of the outbuildings to his son-in-law, William Russell. The new owner named the structure the Mountain House Hotel and installed a telegraph line. As long as stagecoach traffic continued through the Willamette Valley, the hotel provided food, drinks, and lodging to weary travelers. Eventually, the main roads and railroads bypassed Lorane, negating the need for a hostelry, so from 1900 until the 1960s, the Cartwright House served as a residence. [51]

GRANVILLE BABER HOUSE

Some Oregon Greek Revival houses resemble others, most possess distinguishing characteristics of their own, and a few are unique, having virtually nothing in common with the others in the state. The Granville H. Baber House in Linn County near Albany fits the latter criteria. From the front, the Baber House appears tiny, with space for no more than three or four rooms. This angle of view is deceptive,

Figure 5.20: Granville H. Baber House, Albany, Oregon. Built by Granville H. Baber, ca. 1854. *Courtesy Oregon State Parks.*

however, for behind the front block the principal living quarters extend in an S-shape design, with one wing perpendicular to and the other parallel to the main structure. The visual illusion continues on the perpendicular wing, which from the outside looks like a single-story space. Upon closer inspection, it is a story-and-a-half building with a kitchen and dining area on the first floor and two bedrooms upstairs. Together the three interconnected sections provide a remarkably spacious living area.[52]

The designer of the Baber House apparently enjoyed unconventionality. In addition to the unusual building plan, he used stylistic features that were different from most classical houses in Oregon (Figures 5.20–5.21). For example, he placed a delicate portico with a full pediment and four fluted Greek Doric columns on the front facade. Although it was elegant, the porch was asymmetrically located on the structure, with two window bays flanking the south side and one on the north. Classical detailing on the rest of the dwelling, however, demonstrated his sophisticated taste. Pediments matching the

Figure 5.21: Granville H. Baber House, Albany, Oregon. Built by Granville H. Baber, ca. 1854. *Courtesy Oregon State Parks.*

portico adorn the gabled ends on the main structure and on the sides of the wings. A full Tuscan entablature surrounds the main structure, and Roman Doric pilasters support the corners. Within the portico, the craftsmanship equals or surpasses the work on its exterior. Generous moldings and two engaged columns, identical to the portico pillars, encased the entrance. In the doorway itself, two smaller pilasters separated the door and sidelights, and a transom topped the entire ensemble.

Granville Baber listed carpenter as his occupation in the 1850 Oregon census. Thus, he almost certainly designed and built his house, using tools he brought across the plains in 1845. He had the necessary funds to purchase materials as well, for like most of his neighbors, Baber ventured to the California goldfields in 1848, spent three months prospecting on the American River, and returned home in 1849 with a tidy amount of gold dust. He was elected judge of Linn County in 1851. He started building the new house sometime between 1852 and 1854 and, according to a local legend, patterned his new dwelling after the White House.[53] It is more likely, though, that he recalled the appearance of noteworthy structures from his home state of Virginia — such as Arlington House — and used pattern books to design some of the more intricate details.[54] In any case, Baber allowed his imagination free rein in creating the residence, thereby making an important contribution to classical architecture in Oregon.

JOHN PHILLIPS HOUSE

Thirty miles north of the Baber House and near Salem, John Phillips, another carpenter, built his version of a Greek Revival house. Like Baber, Phillips arrived in Oregon in 1845, but unlike his neighbor to the south, Phillips was born in England. He was raised in Wiltshire, apprenticed with a cabinetmaker at the age of eleven, and nine years later decided to emigrate to the United States. During the Atlantic crossing in 1834, Phillips made acquaintance with a minister from Florida and decided to follow his new friend south. He worked for the United States government during the Seminole Wars and in 1839 moved to New Orleans where he married an Englishwoman, Elizabeth Hibbard. After a brief stay in Louisiana, the couple settled in St. Louis, Missouri; then in 1845 the Phillipses departed with the Stephen Meek wagon train for Oregon. Meek unwisely led a large party of 150 to 200 wagons on a dangerous cutoff from Fort Boise across the high desert of central Oregon. As many as seventy-five of those who followed Meek on the shortcut perished. It is not known whether Phillips and his wife followed Meek or continued with the others on the more heavily traveled northern route. In any event, while the Phillipses were crossing the Snake River in Idaho, they lost their team and wagon and barely escaped with their own lives.

When Phillips arrived in Oregon, he soon discovered that his cabinetmaking skills were in great demand. He and a fellow wagon train companion, Thomas Roberts, found steady work building the Roman Catholic church and school in St. Paul. In 1847 Phillips purchased a 640-acre farm near Salem. Then, in the spring of 1849, he and a neighbor went to the goldfields. Two years following his return, he began building a new house. When it was completed in 1853, Phillips started a business making drapes, sashes, blinds, coffins, and furniture. Some of his handiwork remains in the house, which is still owned by his decendants.[55]

Compared with other Greek Revival residences in the Willamette Valley, the classical detailing on the Phillips House is sparse (Figures 5.22–5.23). While the decoration may not be elaborate or extensive, the

147

Figure 5.22: John Phillips House, Salem, Oregon. Built by John Phillips, 1853. *Courtesy Oregon State Parks.*

Figure 5.23: John Phillips House, Salem, Oregon. Built by John Phillips, 1853. *Courtesy Oregon State Parks.*

Figure 5.24: Creole Cottage, New Orleans, Louisiana. Unknown builder, ca. 1830. *Courtesy Christovich et al., eds.*, New Orleans Architecture.

execution and the meticulous craftsmanship throughout are as impressive as the artistry of any 1850s Oregon house. The front veranda supported by six chamferred columns, the double-pitched roof, the narrow cornices, and the overall small size suggest that Phillips's design may have been influenced by the Creole cottages he saw in New Orleans (Figure 5.24).[56] In addition to the molded cornice and Roman Doric caps on the columns, he topped the windows and doorframes with simple pedimented architraves. Phillips, in a significant departure from most other classical houses in Oregon, chose to omit any form of pediment on the gable ends.

Phillips built a modest-sized house for a small family in 1853, but eventually he and his wife had sixteen children, of which eleven lived to maturity. As the family grew, the father was forced to divide and add rooms to accommodate the new members. He built two rooms in the end bays of the front porch, but delineated the new from the old portion by recessing the walls about four inches within the existing cornice and columns. The siding, window surrounds, and pedimented architrave motif matched the original materials and design.[57] This

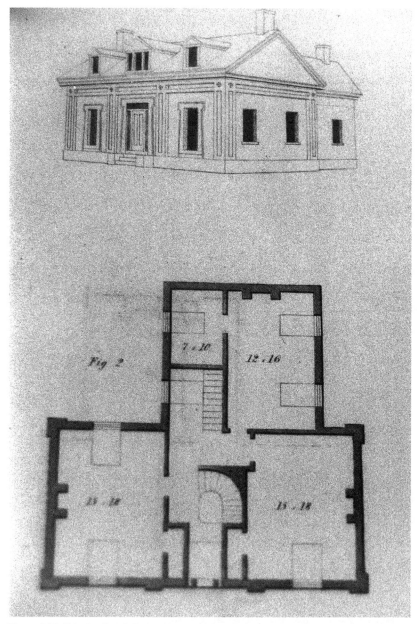

Figure 5.25: Plan for Greek Revival cottage taken from Edward Shaw, *Rural Architecture*, 1843.

Figure 5.26: Jacob Conser House, Jefferson, Oregon. Built by Jacob Conser, 1856. *Courtesy Oregon State Parks.*

Figure 5.27: Jacob Conser House, Jefferson, Oregon. Built by Jacob Conser, 1856. *Courtesy Oregon State Parks.*

early remodeling technique would be considered an excellent rehabilitation treatment today for blending new materials into the old, and for separating the additions by recessing the walls within the original columns and cornice.

JACOB CONSER HOUSE

In the terms of vernacular architecture, Phillips's remodeling job transformed his cottage into a "saddlebag" house — a term derived from the appearance of the enclosed front side bays and the open porch in between.[58] The Jacob Conser House in the small community of Jefferson, Oregon, is another saddlebag classical dwelling. Yet unlike the Phillips House, the builder enclosed the portico in the original design. Conser called himself a carpenter in the 1850 census, and he listed Pennsylvania and Illinois as his earlier residences. He may have copied a structure he had seen in the East or the Midwest, or as Oregon architectural historian Marion Ross suggests, Conser perhaps borrowed the plan from Edward Shaw's handbook, *Rural Architecture* (1843) (Figure 5.25).[59]

Conser developed the recessed portico as the major design element (Figures 5.26–5.27). Two correct Greek Doric columns and matching pilasters gave this feature an almost religious aura. With the exception of the unique entryway, however, the rest of the Conser House was a predictable 1850s Oregon residence. The boxed cornice and plain frieze represented an entablature, and square pilasters on the corners of the two front bays carried the column motif across the front facade. Eave returns on the gable ends suggested pediments, and the molded cornices over some of the windows continued the classical theme. Conser's building plan was practical, consisting of a main body as living quarters for his family and a substantial ell extension that served as a hostel for travelers using the east side roads of the Willamette Valley. The upper story of the ell became a multipurpose room, used for local meetings and social activities, or as an extra sleeping area if the guest list could not be accommodated in the first-floor bedrooms.

In 1937 the City of Jefferson acquired the Conser House as a city hall and public library. The municipality restored and remodeled the house in cooperation with the Works Projects Administration in 1939. Although the restoration removed some interior fabric, it left most of the significant detailing in place. Since 1939 the Conser House has continued to serve as the city hall, a notable architectural monument, and a source of pride for local residents.[60]

AMOS COOK HOUSE

Amos Cook, one of Oregon's early residents, started building his Greek Revival house near Dayton while many of his neighbors were returning from the California goldfields. He had been a member of the Peoria party, which under the leadership of Thomas Jefferson Farnham left the Midwest to settle in Oregon. Farnham and his group of nineteen young men were inspired to embark on their adventure by the Reverend Jason Lee of the Willamette Methodist Mission, who spoke in Peoria. They left Illinois in 1839, carrying a flag with the motto, "Oregon or the Grave." Along the way most of the members of the expedition dropped out, and only eight men arrived in Oregon. Cook was one of the hardy few who finished the journey. He settled on the Yamhill River near Dayton. In some ways Cook's experiences paralleled those of Alvin T. Smith. Both men arrived in Oregon at about the same time, both were carpenters as well as farmers, and both

Figure 5.28: Amos Cook House, Dayton, Oregon. Built by Amos Cook, 1854. *Courtesy Oregon State Parks.*

constructed their own Greek Revival houses. Cook, however, was actively involved in politics, voting to establish a provisional government at Champoeg in 1843.[61]

Cook probably joined other Oregonians who went to the California goldfields. His name was omitted from the 1850 census — although his neighbors were included — which suggests that he was away from his farm for an extended period of time. By 1854 he acquired enough money to build a classical house for his bride, Mary Frances Scott. Their dwelling was not elaborate in size or detailing (Figure 5.28). A simple entablature surrounded the structure with returns at the eaves. The entryway was located in the center of the main facade, but it was plain, lacking the side and transom windows common to most Oregon classical houses of the 1850s. According to his daughter, Cook's creative energies were devoted to the front porch. She stated that her father designed the four unusual sets of uncapped columns with the delicate diagonal braces between each set of pillars. The walls were unusually thick, suggesting two possibilities: either the framing system used heavy timbers or the dwelling was created by converting a hewn-log structure into a Greek Revival house.[62]

Figure 5.29: Francis Fletcher House, Dayton, Oregon. Unknown designer, ca. 1864. *Courtesy Oregon State Parks.*

FRANCIS FLETCHER HOUSE

About ten years after Cook completed his new residence, Francis Fletcher, a neighbor and longtime friend, constructed a house on the adjacent Donation Land Claim. Fletcher was born in England and at the age of fourteen came with his family to Ontario, Canada, and then moved on to Peoria, Illinois. Along with Cook, he was one of the eight young men of the Peoria party who reached Oregon. There he and Cook settled on neighboring farms in the Willamette Valley and remained friends the rest of their lives. Fletcher's house was similar in size and form to his neighbor's dwelling, but stylistically the two structures were quite different.

The Fletcher residence clearly demonstrates a transition from the Greek Revival to a more simplified vernacular style (Figure 5.29). In its dimensions, interior layout, and construction techniques, it lacked any classical detailing. The eave overhangs were broad, without entablatures, returns, or pediments. The corner pilasters were strictly functional, omitting the usual decorative caps.[63] Fletcher's new residence was an anachronism when compared to Amos Cook's house. Both men arrived in Oregon at the same time, both were friends, and both

155

emigrated from Illinois. Given these factors, Fletcher and Cook might well have built houses that looked alike.

Perhaps Fletcher did not admire Greek Revival architecture or could not afford to build a new house when the style was in vogue. Yet his house and other dwellings of the 1860s generally were more functional than decorative, and architectural detailing was attached to rather than incorporated in these structures. Phillip Dole states that mass-produced building components made up major portions of Oregon's residences of the 1860s. Items such as sashes, doors, and blinds came from the planing and sash factories in larger towns throughout the state. These same mills manufactured the gingerbread details prominently displayed on Gothic Revival and Victorian structures in standard sizes.[64] Further, after nearly a decade of sustained growth, the Oregon economy tapered off during the early 1860s, suggesting yet another reason for the change in architectural style.

WOLF CREEK TAVERN

Before Oregonians abandoned Greek Revival architecture altogether, they erected several classical public buildings. The Wolf Creek Tavern, near Grants Pass, has long been regarded as one of Oregon's best Greek Revival buildings. Oral tradition held that the inn was built in 1857 as a major stop on the Oregon and California stagecoach line. Legends further claimed that Presidents Rutherford B. Hayes and Ulysses S. Grant stayed overnight and that Jack London completed his *Valley of the Moon* manuscript at the tavern. During a recent major renovation, a research team finally systematically investigated the hostelry's history. The scholars discovered that it was built at least twenty years later than the traditional date given, that it was not a major stop on the stage line, that it likely was not standing when the presidents traveled through Oregon, and that it may or may not have been a place where Jack London stayed. It gained its significance as a roadhouse when the Pacific Highway passed by its front door in 1914.[65]

Architecturally, the two-story front veranda showcases the principal classical detailing (Figure 2.35). Six square posts on each floor, topped with capitals with pierced railing on the second level to space the columns, accentuated this Greek Revival feature. The boxed cornice, with returns at the gable ends, suggested an entablature and pediment. Shallow pediments over the front windows and doors were the remaining classical details. The interior was arranged around a

Figure 5.30: Pioneer Courthouse, Portland, Oregon. Designed by A. B. Mullet, 1867. *Courtesy Oregon State Parks.*

central stair hall, flanked by identical parlors. The kitchen and dining room occupied the first floor of the ell, and the entire second floor consisted of sleeping rooms. A dormitory wing that was added to the rear of the structure in 1915 blended well with the main block in materials and detailing. The recent restoration has faithfully and taste-fully returned the Wolf Creek Tavern to its orginal appearance.[66]

PORTLAND PIONEER COURTHOUSE

Perhaps the best known of all early public edifices in the Pacific Northwest (at least in the eyes of Portlanders) is the Pioneer Court-house in the center of downtown Portland. When it was constructed in 1867, the citizens of the city complained that the new federal building was too far away from town. At that time, Portland's downtown was located along the waterfront of the Willamette River, and the court-house was about a mile from the major commercial establishments. As the city grew, the courthouse became a prominent part of the city center. In its courtroom venerable Judge Matthew P. Deady heard plead-ings and rendered decisions on major land fraud cases as well as lesser matters. Several presidents, including Ulysses S. Grant, Rutherford B.

Hayes, Benjamin Harrison, Theodore Roosevelt, and William Howard Taft, actually did visit this building and viewed the city from its glass-enclosed cupola. During World War II, entertainers performed on a stage at the west end of the courthouse to encourage the purchase of war bonds. The structure was nearly razed when the federal court moved to a new building in 1933, but preservationists and Federal Judge John Kilkenny prevailed on the General Services Administration to keep and restore the building. The Pioneer Courthouse now houses the Ninth Circuit Court of Appeals of the United States and offices for Oregon's United States senators.

As an architectural monument, the Pioneer Courthouse is a classical structure with a scattering of early Victorian details (Figure 5.30). The pilasters, the full Doric entablature and pediment, and the lantern cupola all combined to give this building its classical vocabulary. Prominent moldings over the first- and second-story windows and the semi-eliptical arches on the street level openings anticipated the Italianate edifices that would appear in Portland within the next twenty years.

A. B. Mullet, a noted government architect, designed the new courthouse. Among his many other masterpieces, the San Francisco Mint and the State, War, and Navy Building in Washington, D.C., were perhaps his best-known works. A recent book notes that Mullet's plan for the Portland courthouse was intended for another federal building in a different city. The architect's drawings were filed away and resurrected when the government decided to construct a courthouse in Portland.[67] Mullet's design, which was actually intended for an eastern city, gave Portland a taste of high style Greek Revival architecture. It also demonstrated the lingering popularity of the style. Except for two wings added on the west end in 1903 that blended with the structure and its surroundings, the Pioneer Courthouse has remained unchanged as a prominent landmark in downtown Portland.

WALLER HALL, WILLAMETTE UNIVERSITY

Just as construction began on the Pioneer Courthouse, Willamette University in Salem was preparing to dedicate its new and most prominent building, Waller Hall. The school was founded in 1842 by Methodist missionaries and in the ensuing years had increased in both size and stature. By 1860 the board of trustees decided to construct a new building to accommodate the growing enrollment. A fund-raising drive collected enough money in four years to begin the project. When

Figure 5.31: Waller Hall, Willamette University, Salem, Oregon. Unknown designer, 1867. *Courtesy Oregon State Parks.*

construction began, the builders discovered that the ground on the site possessed a high clay content, so they built a kiln there and produced the bricks from the earth excavated for the basement.[68]

The Reverend Alvin F. Waller, a longtime Methodist leader, was in charge of fund raising and construction. When the building was completed in 1867, the college trustees honored him by naming it Waller Hall. The building became the main classroom and administration offices for the university, as well as a community center for Salem (Figure 5.31). A year after its completion, pioneer historian Gustavus Hines described the structure:

> The plan of the building is that of a Greek cross, and was recommended by Bishop Janes when he last visited the Oregon conference. The two parts of the cross are each eighty-four feet long and forty-four feet wide. These cross each other exactly in the center, so that the building presents about the same appearance from whichever side you take your observation. . . . There are three entrances to the building, the main entrance into the chapel being in the end of the north wing, and other entrances being in the east and west wings. . . . The chapel is very commodious, occupying the entire story of the cross above the basement, running north and south. . . . It is nicely finished with a broad platform at the south end, and finely and comfortably seated throughout. At each side there is a door which passes into the east and west wings to the stairways. One of these doors is designed for the ingress and egress of the ladies, and the other for the gentlemen of the school. The school rooms in the second and third stories are large and very neatly finished . . . with seats of the latest improvement. They are of sufficient capacity to accommodate about four hundred pupils.[69]

The facades of the wings were each divided into three bays with Doric-capped pilasters. Each end of the cross was accentuated by full pediments with simple entablatures. Paired, roundheaded windows were set within the semicircular openings in each pediment, and the first- and second-story windows were surmounted with brick-denticulated lintels. Early photographs show three simple porticoed entrances — scaled-down images of the gable pediments with identical detailing.[70]

By 1859 Alvin T. Smith and about forty others had completed their Greek Revival houses; that same year, Oregon became a state. Oregonians built a relatively small number of classical houses compared to states in the East, Midwest, and South. And the sizes, appearances, and plans of the Oregon residences differed considerably. Most resembled examples from the Midwest, though some looked like southern mansions and others like New England dwellings. These houses were evidence of economic prosperity, because so many of their owners had been successful during the California gold rush. The carpenters who built these residences undoubtedly were familiar with Greek Revival architecture in other regions of the country. They also had the proper tools to execute the classical detailing. Some used pattern books while others worked from memory. Together the owners and carpenters made tangible contributions to Oregon's architectural legacy.

6

Epilogue

In 1866 Alvin T. Smith returned to Connecticut. Over the years he had corresponded with his family, but he had not seen New England for over thirty years. Although Smith did not give a reason for the visit, he seemed to have had a powerful desire to return to his roots. Also, his wife had died eight years earlier, which probably increased his resolve to visit his family one more time. He stayed for about two years, during which time he married a second wife, Jane Averill.[1] After his visit, he and his new bride returned to his farm and Greek Revival house in Oregon, where he lived until his death in 1887 at the age of eighty-five.

Few pioneers returned home after such long absences. Smith's attachment to the East was so strong, he was drawn back, although his age and the long, grueling distance made the journey difficult. Yet even though he returned to Connecticut and married a native New Englander, he did not stay there. He embarked on an equally arduous trip back to Oregon. In other words, the West exerted an even stronger pull on Smith than the Northeast.

As Smith made a commitment to stay in Oregon and devote his energies toward building a new state, the same was true for nearly all of Oregon's other Greek Revival house owners. Most Oregon pioneers endured considerable hardships, seeking better lives in several places before settling in Oregon. Their journey was now over. They were satisfied that they had found the promised land. Yet while Oregonians took many risks in finding their garden of Eden, once they settled there, they sought ways to duplicate lives they had known in the East. They continued in their livelihoods as farmers, maintained their familiar customs, and built houses that reminded them of home. In short, they were conservative and slow to accept change.[2]

The next generation of Oregonians proved more adventuresome in selection of house styles. Although they, for the most part, had not seen built examples of the now-popular Gothic Revival style, they

Figure 6.1: Fort Dalles Surgeon's Quarters, The Dalles, Oregon. Unknown designer, 1856. *Courtesy Oregon State Parks.*

instructed their builders to use plates from pattern books to construct these modern houses. Andrew Jackson Downing's *The Architecture of Country Houses* (1850) provided the model and inspiration for one of Oregon's most interesting examples of this style, the Fort Dalles Surgeon's Quarters in The Dalles (Figure 6.1–6.2).[3] Similar sources stimulated the development of other Romantic styles in the state as well.

Oregon's Greek Revival houses represented the final manifestations of the style in the United States. This style, which started in Europe, flourished in the eastern United States, and culminated in Oregon, signaled the renewed interest in the antiquities, the establishment of the American architectural profession, the popularity of pattern books, and the desire of Americans to build stylistic structures. From the Second Bank of the United States in Philadelphia to the Alvin T. Smith House in Oregon, American architects and carpenters exhibited their interpretations of classical architecture. Although some structures were stately, with sophisticated detailing, and others were simple, with little ornamentation, as a whole, the American Greek Revival style made a clear statement that the country had reached a plateau of cultural maturity.

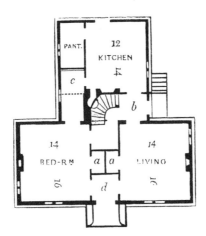

Figure 6.2: Plate taken from Andrew Jackson Downing, *The Architecture of Country Houses*, 1850.

GLOSSARY

Acanthus: A thistlelike plant. The Greeks copied the leaves for Corinthian capitals.

Anthemion: A stylized honeysuckle flower motif used for architectural ornamentation.

Architrave: Either the lowest member of a full entablature, or sometimes used by itself to enframe a window.

Bay: The portion of a structure divided by columns or pilasters. A projecting section of a building, usually called a bay window.

Boxed cornice: The decorative section directly under the eaves used to represent an entablature. Differs from an entablature.

Cantilevered: A type of construction usually represented by a substantial overhang. A beam or series of beams are supported by downward pressure.

Cap: Same as capital.

Capital: The top part of a column or pilaster.

Chamfer: Where two corners meet and the sharp edge is cut away and beveled.

Clapboard: Overlapping exterior wallboards attached horizontally and tapered to facilitate placement on the wall and provide weatherproofing.

Column: A vertical support member. For the Greek Revival style, most columns have three parts — base, shaft, and capital.

Corinthian: The most elaborate classical order, distinguished by the acanthus leaf capitals.

Cornice: The uppermost part of an entablature, or the plain decoration under the eaves.

Cupola: A small domed feature adorning the top of a structure.

Cyma recta: A type of molding typical in Greek Revival houses. It is distinguished by a reversed curve with the convex portion near the wall.

Cyma reversa: Different from the **cyma recta** mold in that the concave half is near the wall.

Dentil: Typical of Ionic order architecture. The dentils are small blocklike projections that form a molding as part of an entablature.

Dogtrot: Breezeway portion of a double house that divides both blocks.

Doric: A classical order that is distinguished by its simplicity. Unornamented captials and metopes and triglyphs on the entablature distinguish this order.

Glossary

Dovetail joint: A corner joint where the protruding section, looking like a dove's tail, fits into a slot.

Eave: The edge of a roof that projects over a wall.

Engaged column: Decorative exterior framework supporting the corners or dividing the bays. For classical revival structures, an order is represented on this feature. Synonymous with pilaster.

Entablature: A horizontal portion of a classical structure between the eaves and the columns. A correct entablature is distinguished with an architrave on the bottom, a frieze in the middle, and a cornice on top. Further, the entablature varies depending on the particular order used on the structure.

Entasis: A Greek technique used to correct optical illusions on classical structures. In some instances the columns are slightly curved near the top to give a uniform appearance from a distance. In other cases the spaces between pillars are varied slightly, making them appear perfectly spaced when viewed from a distant vantage point.

Fenestration: The placement of openings (principally windows) on a facade.

Finial: The top of a gable, spire, or cupola.

Fluting: The grooves or simulated curves on classical columns or pilasters.

Fret: A band that ornaments a molding.

Frieze: The middle part of an entablature or a relief sculpture decorating a feature such as the pediment.

Gable: A roof type, typical of most classical structures, which is distinguished by its triangular shape.

Hipped roof: A roof that slopes on all sides with the lines meeting at the top corners.

Ionic: A classical order distinguished by the scroll design on the column capital.

Lintel: A beam spanning an opening (door or window) and supported by columns or vertical beams.

Massing: The grouping of individual building components to make a unified whole.

Metopes: The blank spaces between the triglyphs in a Doric order entablature.

Modillion: A small bracket used to support the upper member of a Corinthian entablature.

Mortise: The cutout portion of a joint designed to receive the tenon.

Order: The structural system of classical architecture. Consists of building components, such as entablature, columns, pediment, and the detailing, which are Doric, Ionic, or Corinthian. On the various vernacular manifestations of the style, orders often were mixed, or in some instances, builders used Roman Tuscan or other orders.

Parapet: A side wall that extends above the roof line.

Pediment: The gable end of a structure, triangular in shape. On some of the vernacular classical houses, returns at the eaves often represented a pediment.

Peristyle: A colonade surrounding the outside of a structure.

Pilaster: A column on the corners or dividing the bays. The classical order is represented on this feature.

Portico: A substantial porch on the front of a classical structure with columns and a pediment.

Renaissance Revival: An architectural style with roots in ancient Rome and popularized by buildings constructed in fifteenth-century Italy. These buildings generally are characterized by elaborate detailing and vaulted domes.

Return: A typical feature on vernacular classical houses. The entablature extends around the sides of the structure to represent a pediment.

Ribs: The arches within a vault used to support the structure.

Rotunda-dome-wing plan: A plan popularized with the National Capitol and used on nearly all statehouses throughout the country. The rotunda and dome are situated at the center and flanked by wings for the House of Representatives and Senate.

Sill beam: A major structural member on many early wooden houses. A large timber is cut and horizontally placed on stone or rock piers, and vertical framing is attached to it.

Sunburst: An architectural detail made popular by the sixteenth-century Italian designer Andrea Palladio. The sunburst is usually a semicircular window and is often referred to as a Palladian window.

Tenon: The projecting portion of a joint that fits snugly into a mortise.

Transom: An opening over a door or window made of wood or glass and designed for ventilation.

Triglyphs: The projecting blocks in the entablature of the Doric order interspersed with metopes.

Tuscan: A simple order from ancient Rome that is similar to the Doric order, except the capital is more pronounced, the columns usually are not fluted, and the entablature does not feature metopes and triglyphs.

Vault: A rounded structural feature supported with arches and constructed of stone, brick, concrete, or sometimes wood.

Vernacular: A style adapted to reflect the needs of a local area, or simplified because of materials, equipment, or the limited knowledge of the builder.

Glossary

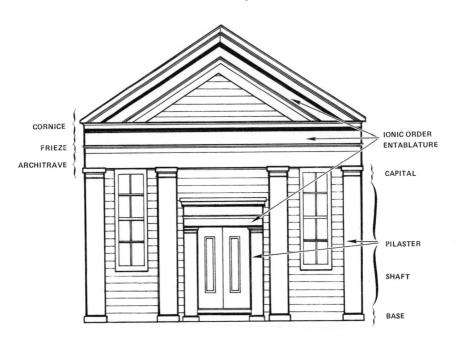

CORNICE
FRIEZE
ARCHITRAVE

IONIC ORDER ENTABLATURE

CAPITAL

PILASTER

SHAFT

BASE

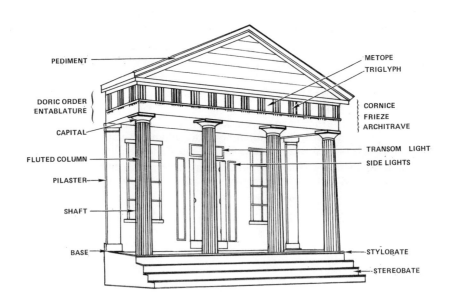

PEDIMENT

METOPE
TRIGLYPH

DORIC ORDER ENTABLATURE

CAPITAL

CORNICE
FRIEZE
ARCHITRAVE

FLUTED COLUMN

TRANSOM LIGHT
SIDE LIGHTS

PILASTER

SHAFT

BASE

STYLOBATE
STEREOBATE

Glossary

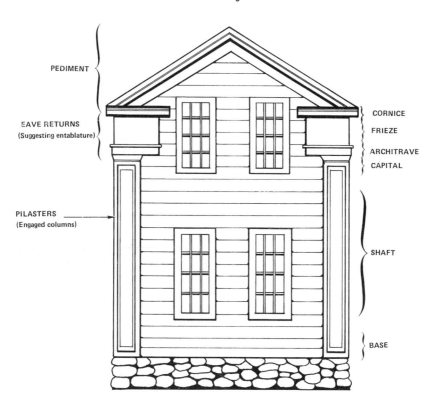

PEDIMENT

EAVE RETURNS
(Suggesting entablature)

PILASTERS
(Engaged columns)

CORNICE

FRIEZE

ARCHITRAVE

CAPITAL

SHAFT

BASE

NOTES

CHAPTER 1

1.   Alvin T. Smith Collection, MSS 8, Manuscript Collection, Oregon Historical Society, Portland, hereafter cited as Smith Diary.

2.   Philip Dole, who has spent many years studying Oregon's pioneer architecture, presents this comparison of Applegate and Waldo in his essay "Farmhouses and Barns in the Willamette Valley," in Thomas Vaughan and Virginia Guest Ferriday, eds., *Space, Style, and Structure: Building in Northwest America*, 2 vols. (Portland: Oregon Historical Society, 1974), 2:79–81. In addition to this article, Marion Dean Ross has written on early Oregon architecture in *A Century of Architecture in Oregon, 1859–1959* (Portland: Oregon Chapter of the American Institute of Architects, 1959) and "Architecture in Oregon, 1845–1895," *Oregon Historical Quarterly* 57 (March 1956): 1–47. Another earlier source on Pacific Northwest architecture is Thomas R. Garth, Jr., "Early Architecture in the Northwest," *Pacific Northwest Quarterly* 38 (January 1947): 215–32.

3.   Frederick Douglass, *My Bondage and My Freedom* (New York: Miller, Orton, and Mulligan, 1855), 67.

4.   Dora Wiebenson, *Sources of Greek Revival Architecture* (London: A. Zwemmer, Ltd., 1969); J. J. Coulton, *Ancient Architects at Work: Problems of Structure and Design* (Ithaca, N.Y.: Cornell University Press, 1977).

5.   Talbot Hamlin, *Greek Revival Architecture in America: Being an Account of Important Trends in American Architecture and American Life Prior to the War Between the States* (New York: Oxford University Press, 1944), p. 317.

6.   Roger G. Kennedy, *Greek Revival America* (New York: Stewart, Tabori, and Chang, 1989).

7.   In his discussion of Greek Revival architecture in Oregon, Hamlin uses only one example, the Dr. John McLoughlin House in Oregon City. Actually the McLoughlin House was not Greek Revival at all, but a French-Canadian I-house. Hamlin, *Greek Revival Architecture*, 312. Kennedy also includes the McLoughlin House as the only notable classical building in Oregon. Kennedy, *Greek Revival America*, 417.

8.   Dell Upton and John Michael Vlach have collected a superb selection of essays on vernacular architecture in *Common Places: Readings in American Vernacular Architecture* (Athens: University of Georgia Press, 1986). In addition, I have found the following sources to be useful as well: Henry Glassie, *Folk Building in Middle Virginia: A Structural Analysis of Historical Artifacts* (Knoxville: University of Tennessee Press, 1975); Glassie's *Pattern in the Material Folk Culture of the Eastern United States* (Philadelphia: University of Pennsylvania Press, 1968); and Camille Wells, *Perspectives in Vernacular Architecture II* (Columbia: University of Missouri Press, 1986).

9.   Fred B. Kniffen, "Louisiana House Types," *Annals of the Association of American Geographers* 26 (1936): 179–93. Some of the more important works by geographers on the subject of settlement patterns are: Fred Kniffen and Henry Glassie, "Building in Wood in the Eastern United States: A Time-Place Perspective," *Geographical*

Review 66 (March 1966): 40–66; Henry Glassie, "The Types of the Southern Mountain Cabin," in Jan Brunvand, ed., *The Study of American Folklore* (New York: W. W. Norton and Company, 1968); Glassie, *Folk Building in Middle Virginia*; Glassie, "Eighteenth-Century Cultural Process in Delaware Valley Folk Building," *Winterthur Portfolio* 7 (Autumn 1972): 29–57; Howard Wright Marshall, *Folk Architecture in Little Dixie: A Regional Culture in Missouri* (Columbia: University of Missouri Press, 1981); and Jennifer Eastman Attebery, "The Square Cabin: A Folk House Type in Idaho," *Idaho Yesterdays* 26 (September 1982): 25–31.

10. Fred B. Kniffen, "Folk Housing: Key to Diffusion," *Annals of the Association of American Geographers* 55 (December 1965): 549–77.

11. Dell Upton, "Pattern Books and Professionalism: Aspects of the Transformation of Domestic Architecture in America, 1800–1860," *Winterthur Portfolio* 19 (Autumn 1984): 107–50.

12. Among the sources that chronicle the changes in historical interpretation in the West are: Michael P. Malone, ed., *Historians and the American West* (Lincoln: University of Nebraska Press, 1983); Malone and Rodman W. Paul, "Tradition and Challange in Western Historiography," *Western Historical Quarterly* 16 (1985): 27–53; W. Turrentine Jackson, "A Brief Message for the Young and/or Ambitious: Comparative Frontiers as a Field for Investigation," *Western Historical Quarterly* 9 (1978): 5–18; and Jerome O. Steffen, *Comparative Frontiers: A Proposal for Studying the American West* (Norman: University of Oklahoma Press, 1980). Also see W. N. Davis, Jr., "Will the West Survive as a Field in American History? A Survey Report," *Mississippi Valley Historical Review* 50 (March 1964): 672–85; Gene M. Gressley, ed., *The American West: A Reorientation*, University of Wyoming Publications 32 (Laramie: University of Wyoming Press, 1966); and Rodman W. Paul, "The Mormons as a Theme in Western Historical Writing," *Journal of American History* 54 (December 1967): 511–23. Western studies are undergoing a major revisionist movement, led by Patricia Nelson Limerick's *The Legacy of Conquest: The Unbroken Past of the American West* (New York: W. W. Norton and Company, 1987). The work of Limerick and others is analyzed in Richard Bernstein's "Unsettling the Old West" in *New York Times Magazine* (18 March 1990), 34–35, 56–57, 59.

13. In a recent special issue of the *Pacific Historical Review*, which focused on architecture and the American West, the contributors indicated that, as a trend, early western architecture usually was similar to the styles from the settled regions, whereas more recent designs tended to be more creative. Robert W. Rydell, ed., "Architecture and the American West" (A Special Issue), *Pacific Historical Review* 54 (November 1985). Other authors who have written about the architecture of the West are as follows: Harold Kirker, "California Architecture and Its Relation to Contemporary Trends in Europe and America," *California Historical Quarterly* 51 (March 1972): 289–305, and *California's Architectural Frontier: Style and Tradition in the Nineteenth Century* (San Marino, Calif.: Huntington Library, 1960; reprint ed. Salt Lake City: University of Utah Press, 1973); and Robert Winter, "Architecture on the Frontier: The Mormon Experiment," *Pacific Historical Review* 43 (March 1974): 50–60.

14. Thomas Schlereth has defined the use of material culture by historians in his *Artifacts and the American Past* (Nashville: AASLH, 1980), 4–5. Schlereth also has edited *Material Culture Studies in America* (Nashville: AASLH, 1982) and *American Quarterly* 35 (1983): 236–338. The latter is an entire issue devoted to a bibliography of material culture studies. Other useful sources on material culture are: M. G. Quimby, ed., *Material Culture and the Study of American Life* (New York: W. W. Norton and Company, 1978); Ivor Noel Hume, *Historical Archeology* (New York: Alfred A. Knopf, 1969); J. C. Harrington, "Archeology as an Auxiliary to American History," *American Anthropologist* 57 (December 1955): 1121–30; and Leland Fergu-

son, ed., *Historical Archeology and the Importance of Material Things* (New York: Chelsea House Publishers, 1968).

15. The National Register of Historic Places is housed in the United States Department of the Interior, National Park Service, Washington, D.C. The Historic American Building Survey is housed in the Library of Congress, Washington, D.C. These sources document structures nationwide and include photographs. They do not, however, include building plans for all structures, and thus limit the researcher's ability to determine building types.

16. The following works have been particularly helpful in shaping my architectural history methodology: Spiro Kostof, *A History of Architecture: Settings and Rituals* (New York: Oxford University Press, 1985); J. Mordaunt Crook, *The Dilemma of Style: Architectural Ideals from the Picturesque to the Post-Modern* (Chicago: University of Chicago Press, 1987); David Wadkin, *The Rise of Architectural History* (London: Architectural Press, 1981); Berel Lang, *The Concept of Style* (Philadelphia: University of Pennsylvania Press, 1979); and Juan Pablo Bonta, *Architecture and Its Interpretations* (Cambridge, Mass.: MIT Press, 1986). For the interdisciplinary study of architecture and history, I have found Giles B. Gunn, *The Culture of Criticism and the Criticism of Culture* (New York: Oxford University Press, 1987) to be a useful volume.

CHAPTER 2

1. Examples from the Branford vicinity are taken from "Connecticut Houses," compiled by the Connecticut Society of Colonial Dames of America. Hartford: Connecticut State Library, Bulletin #17, 1942. Also, the National Register Nominations for the Branford Point Historic District and the Branford Center Historic District provided further information. National Register of Historic Places, Inventory — Nomination Form, entered 1984, 1988, on file in the United States of the Interior, National Park Service, Washington, D.C., hereafter cited as National Register, NPS, date of entry.

2. H. C. Hatfield, *Winkelmann and his German Critics 1755–1781: A Prelude to the Classical Age* (New York, 1943).

3. James Stuart and Nicolas Revett, *The Antiquities of Athens*, 4 vols. (London: J. Harberkorn, 1762–1816); Wiebenson, *Sources of Greek Revival*, passim.

4. Coulton, *Ancient Architects*, passim

5. Kennedy, *Greek Revival America*, 5–6; Kostof, *History of Architecture*, 618; Wiebensen, *Sources of Greek Revival*, passim.

6. Talbot Hamlin, *Benjamin Henry Latrobe* (New York: Oxford University Press, 1955), 55. During the period of the Enlightenment in Europe and the United States, gentlemen often combined several interests in their professions. Thomas Jefferson was a farmer, a philosopher, a scientist, an architect, a politician, and a lawyer. While he was an unusual man, the combination of vocations and avocations with such variety was not uncommon during this period. In Europe, some designers practiced as either an architect or an engineer, but in most instances they were both. They received architectural training to understand the aesthetics and functions of a structure and engineering training to learn how a structure worked and how it should be put together. Latrobe was highly skilled in both disciplines. He could build an attractive and complicated structure or a sophisticated water system.

7. Talbot Hamlin, "Some Greek Revival Architects of Philadelphia," *Pennsylvania Magazine of History and Biography* 65 (April 1941): 122; Fiske Kimball, "The Bank of Pennsylvania, an Unknown Masterpiece of American Classicism," *Architectural Record* 43 (August 1918): 132–39; Talbot Hamlin, "Benjamin Henry Latrobe: The

Man and the Architect," *The Maryland Historical Magazine* 38 (January 1943): 343–44.

8. Benjamin Henry Latrobe, *The Journals of Latrobe: Being Notes and Sketches of an Architect, Naturalist, and Traveler in the United States from 1796 to 1820* (New York: D. Appleton and Company, 1905), 139.

9. Hamlin, *Latrobe*, 165–67; Costen Fitz-Gibbon, "Latrobe and the Centre Square Pump House," *Architectural Record* 52 (July 1927): 19–22.

10. Latrobe described the water system and the difficulties he encountered in its construction in his *Journals*. He also provided one of the best early accounts of life and architecture in New Orleans in this same source. Latrobe, *Journals*, 152–269.

11. Murray H. Nelligan, *Lee Mansion: National Memorial*, U.S. Department of the Interior, National Park Service Historical Series #6 (Washington, D.C.: Government Printing Office, n.d.).

12. Mills prepared a drawing for the final facade of Monticello in about 1803, and it is perhaps the best original exterior plan still in existence. H. M. Pierce Gallagher, *Robert Mills: Architect of the Washington Monument* (New York: Columbia University Press, 1935), 4–11.

13. Rhodri Windsor Liscombe, *The Church Architecture of Robert Mills* (Easley, S.C.: Southern Historical Press, 1985), 9–10; John M. Bryan, ed., *Robert Mills: Architect* (Washington, D.C.: AIA Press, 1989), 35–74; Gallagher, *Robert Mills*, 77–78, 217–18.

14. Edward Teitelman and Richard W. Longstreth, *Architecture in Philadelphia: A Guide* (Cambridge, Mass.: MIT Press, 1981), 30, 65; Kenneth Ames, "Robert Mills and the Philadephia Row House," *Journal of the Society of Architectural Historians* 27 (May 1968): 140–46.

15. William H. Pierson, Jr., *American Buildings and Their Architects: The Colonial and Neoclassical Styles* (Garden City, N.Y.: Doubleday and Company, Inc., 1970), 379–80.

16. Gallagher, *Robert Mills*, 165–66; Pierson, *American Building*, 386–87.

17. Marquis James, *The Life of Andrew Jackson* (New York: Garden City Publishing Company, 1938), 577. In 1834 the Hermitage burned and Talbot Hamlin suggests that Andrew Jackson consulted with Robert Mills on the reconstruction plans. See Hamlin, *Greek Revival Architecture*, 239. There is a fairly large amount of correspondence between Jackson, his family, and the builders relating to the work on the Hermitage, but there is no reference to Robert Mills or any architect in this material. John Bassett, ed., *Correspondence of Andrew Jackson*, 7 vols. (Washington, D.C.: Carnegie Institute, 1927–35), 3:310, 313–17, 322–23.

18. Bryan, *Robert Mills*, 107–42; Pierson, *American Building*, 408.

19. Gallagher, *Robert Mills*, 68.

20. Robert Mills to the Committee of the Bunker Hill Monument, 25 March 1825, Talbot Hamlin Collection, Avery Architecture Library, Columbia University, New York.

21. Quoted in Oliver W. Larkin, *Art and Life in America* (New York: Holt, Rinehart, and Winston, 1960), 166.

22. Agnes Addison Gilchrist, *William Strickland, Architect and Engineer: 1788–1854* (Philadelphia: University of Pennsylvania Press, 1950), 1–2; Hamlin, *Latrobe*, 216.

23. *Philadelphia Gazette and Daily Advertiser*, 12 May 1818.

24. Gilchrist, *William Strickland*, 54. An interesting controversy among architectural historians occurred several years ago over exactly who prepared the final plans for the Second Bank of the United States. Fiske Kimball and Talbot Hamlin were of the opinion that Latrobe actually designed the building and Strickland somehow copied the essential elements of the plan, submitted his version of Latrobe's design, won the competition, and served as the supervising architect. Agnes Addison

Gilchrist, on the other hand, studied Latrobe's original plan (which is extant), compared it with the final appearance and configuration of the building, reviewed contemporary newspaper articles, letters, and other accounts, and determined that the final structure was designed by Strickland. Her evidence and analysis of the problem is much more convincing. Fiske Kimball, "The Bank of the United States, 1818–1824," *Architectural Record* 58 (December 1925): 581–94; Hamlin, *Latrobe*, 501; Agnes Addison Gilchrist, "Latrobe vs. Strickland," *Journal of the Society of Architectural Historians* 2 (July 1942): 26–29; Gilchrist, *William Strickland*, 3–5, 53–57.

25. Ibid, p. 55.

26. August Levasseur, *Lafayette in America, 1824–1825*, 2 vols. (Philadelphia: Carey, Lea, and Carey, 1829), 1:151. Frances M. Trollope was impressed with the architecture of Philadelphia, and she made special note of the "white marble [banks that were designed] after Grecian models." *Domestic Manners of the Americans* (London: Whitaker, Trecher, and Company, 1832), 79. Yet another visitor, Bernhard of Saxe-Weimar, wrote that the Second Bank was "the most beautiful building that I have seen in this country." Quoted in Gilchrist, *William Strickland*, 56.

27. Quoted in Kimball, "Bank of the United States," 594.

28. Bray Hammond, "The Second Bank of the United States," *Transactions of the American Philosophical Society* 43 (March 1953): 82; Bray Hammond, *Banks and Politics in America, From the Revolution to the Civil War* (Princeton, N.J.: Princeton University Press, 1957), 312–14.

29. Hamlin, *Greek Revival Architecture*, 277.

30. Smith Burnham, comp., *The First National Bank of West Chester of Chester County, Pennsylvania, 1814–1914*, (n.p., n.d.). Some of the extant Bank of Indiana branches are discussed in greater detail in Chapter 3.

31. Nell Savage Mahoney, "William Strickland and the Building of Tennessee's Capitol, 1845–1854," *Tennessee Historical Quarterly* 4 (June 1945): 99–153. In defense of William Strickland, the tower was completed by his son Francis, and it appears that the scale for the cupola was enlarged. An unsubstantiated legend suggests that the elder Strickland fought hard to delete the tower from the plan to maintain the classical proportions of the building. Gilchrist, *William Strickland*, 15–16.

32. Kennedy, *Greek Revival America*, 185–86, 194–95; Hamlin, *Greek Revival Architecture*, 81–88.

33. John Haviland and Hugh Beaufort, *The Builder's Assistant*, 3 vols. (Philadelphia: John Bloren, 1818–1821).

34. Edward Clark, "The Capitol With Some Notice of Its Architects," in U.S. Congress, House, *Documentary History of the Construction and Development of the United States Capitol Building and Grounds*, House Report 646, 58th Cong. 2d Sess., 1904, pp. 12, 23. Some of the contemporary criticisms are presented in Henry-Russell Hitchcock and William Seale, *Temples of Democracy: The State Capitols of the USA* (New York: Harcourt, Brace, and Jovanovich, 1976), 121–23.

35. Hamlin, *Latrobe*, 257–58.

36. Correspondence relating to the capitol building demonstrates that structural difficulties were observed before the work was under way, and the documents between 1792 and 1803 continually refer to the inadequacies of Thornton's design. *Documentary History of the Capitol*, 24–102.

37. Quoted in Paul F. Norton, "Latrobe, Jefferson and the National Capitol" (Ph.D. diss., Princeton University, 1952), 262. The first appropriation for repairs and alterations to the capitol and other federal structures in Washington was $50,000. This amount was spent quickly to correct mistakes and to make the building sound. Ibid., passim.

38. Eugene Ashton, "The Latrobe Corn-Stalk Columns," *The Magazine of American History* 18 (August 1887): 128–29; Norton, "Latrobe, Jefferson, and the National Capitol," 245–47; Hamlin, *Latrobe*, 267–69.

39. Roger Newton Hale, *Town and Davis, Architects: Pioneers in American Revivalist Architecture* (New York: Columbia University Press, 1942), 19.

40. Davis's name was not mentioned in any of the official documents relating to the Indiana or any other state capitols. Ibid., 87. Fortunately, Davis's role in these buildings is documented in his surviving Day Book. A. J. Davis, Day Book, Davis Papers, Avery Architecture Library, Columbia University, New York.

41. Hale, *Town and Davis*, 160; Hitchcock and Seale, *Temples of Democracy*, 87–88.

42. Davis later became an important architect in the American Gothic Revival style, and he thus was one of the few designers to work successfully in two major styles. Hale, *Town and Davis*, 311–15. Hale suggests that Town and Davis were the major architects for the Illinois and Ohio statehouses. The Illinois Capitol was designed by John Rague, and there is little evidence to suggest that Town or Davis provided anything more than inspiration for this building. Davis was the second architect involved in the Ohio Capitol, and his sketches were partially adopted. The third and final designer, Nathan B. Relly, drastically altered Davis's ideas and used his own concepts to complete the structure. Ibid., 161–66; Old State Capitol, Springfield, Sangaman County, Illinois, National Register, NPS, entered 1977; Ohio Statehouse, Columbus, Franklin County, Ohio, National Register, NPS, entered 1973.

43. Capitol Commission to Governor William A. Palmer, 29 May 1833, *Journals of the House of Representatives*, 21st Sess. (Montpelier: State of Vermont), 31.

44. Mary Greene Nye, *Vermont's State House* (Montpelier: Vermont Publicity Service, 1936), 3.

45. "The Vermont State House," *American Magazine of Useful Knowledge* 3 (1836): 210.

46. Hamlin, *Greek Revival Architecture*, 106–7.

47. Nye, *Vermont State House*, 4–5; Vermont Statehouse, Montpelier, Washington County, Vermont, National Register, NPS, entered 1970.

48. Hitchcock and Seale, *Temples of Democracy*, 93; Old Statehouse, Little Rock, Pulaski County, Arkansas, National Register, NPS, entered 1969.

49. Hitchcock and Seale, *Temples of Democracy*, 95.

50. Ibid., 99–101; Florida State Capitol, Tallahassee, Leon County, Florida, National Register, NPS, entered 1973.

51. As Greek Revival architecture moved West and as carpenters rather than architects began designing these structures, they began to take on more vernacular characteristics. Hitchcock and Seale, *Temples of Democracy*, 101–2; Benicia Capitol-Courthouse, Benicia, Solano County, California, National Register, NPS, entered 1971.

52. Dorothy O. Johansen and Charles M. Gates, *Empire of the Columbia: A History of the Pacific Northwest*, 2d ed. (New York: Harper and Row, Publishers, 1967), 188–90. For a more complete account of the issues and the formation of the provisional government, see 178–94.

53. Saundra Moore, "Oregon's First Capitols, 1853–1876," *Marion County History* 5 (1959): 13.

54. Oregon Territorial Legislative Assembly, *Report of the Commissioners Appointed to Superintend the Erection of Public Buildings at the Seat of Government*, 5th Sess. (22 December 1853), 123–36.

55. *Salem* (Oregon) *Statesman*, 12 December 1854, 18 December 1855.

56. F. G. Young, "Financial History of Oregon, 1849–1859," *Oregon Historical Quarterly* 8 (March 1907): 149–50.

57. *Salem* (Oregon) *Statesman*, 29 January 1856; Moore, "Oregon's First Capitols," 14.

58. Oregon Territorial Assembly, *Report of Commissioners of Public Buildings*, 137.

59. James D. Richardson, ed., *A Compilation of the Messages and Papers of Presidents, 1789–1897*, 12 vols. (Washington, D.C.: Government Printing Office, 1898), 2:193.

60. Everett suggested that the Greeks were establishing an example for other repressed countries to follow by rebelling against the Turks. Edward Everett, ed., "Anastasius; or the Memoirs of a Greek," *North American Review* 11 (October 1820): 280.

61. A. Koreas, ed., "The Ethics of Aristotle," trans. and reviewed by Edward Everett, *North American Review* 17 (October 1823): 392, 415–16, 420.

62. Edward M. Earle, "American Interest in the Greek Cause, 1821–1827," *American Historical Review* 11 (October 1927): 53.

63. Ibid., 54–56; Myrtle A. Cline, "American Attitude Toward the Greek War of Independence, 1821–1828" (Ph.D. diss., Columbia University, 1930), 64–68.

64. Hamlin, *Greek Revival Architecture*, 101.

65. Robert Mills to the Committee on the Bunker Hill Monument, 25 March 1825, Manuscript Collection, Avery Architecture Library, Columbia University, New York.

66. William Wheildon, *Memoir of Solomon Willard* (Boston: Monument Association, 1865).

67. Hamlin, *Greek Revival Architecture*, 101–2, 112–13.

68. William Havard Eliot, *A Description of the Tremont House with Architectural Illustrations* (Boston: Gray and Bowen, 1830), intro.

69. The *North American Review*, a good barometer for American interest in the Greek Revolution as well as classical architecture, seldom mentioned modern Greece after 1828. Hamlin, *Greek Revival Architecture*, 107, 117.

70. Arthur Gilman, *North American Review* 58 (April 1844): 440–63.

71. Hamlin, *Greek Revival Architecture*, 162, 167.

72. Nantucket Historic District, Nantucket, Nantucket County, Massachusetts, National Historic Landmark, NPS, entered 1966.

73. Clay Lancaster, *The Architecture of Historic Nantucket* (New York: McGraw-Hill, 1972), 121–22.

74. One of the businesses associated with this industry was the prefabrication of new dwellings. An early residence in Oregon, the Morton McCarver House in Oregon City, was a "ready-made" structure, shipped around the Horn from Maine to Oregon. Morton McCarver House, Oregon City, Clackamas County, Oregon, National Register, NPS, entered 1974.

75. Broadway Street Historic District, Bangor, Penobscot County, Maine, National Register, NPS, entered 1977.

76. Joyce K. Bibber, *A Home for Everyone: The Greek Revival and Maine Domestic Architecture* (Lanham, Md.: AASLH Press, 1989). Maine's classical architecture is described in *Maine Catalogue: A List of Measured Drawings, Photographs, and Written Documents in the Historical American Building Survey* (Augusta: Maine State Museum, 1974), 80–102. The catalogue pays particular attention to the works of carpenters in the state.

77. Dell Upton, "Pattern Books and Professionalism: Aspects of the Transformation of Domestic Architecture in America, 1800–1860," *Winterthur Portfolio* 19 (Autumn 1984): 107–50.

78. Asher Benjamin, *American Builder's Companion*, 6th ed. (Boston: R. P. and C. Williams, 1826; reprint ed. New York: Dover Publications, 1969), vi–vii.

79. *The Country Builder's Assistant* (Greenfield, Mass.: Thomas Dickman, 1797); *The American Builder's Companion* (Boston: Etheridge and Bliss, 1806); *The Rudiments of Architecture* (Boston: Munroe and Francis, 1814).

80. Benjamin, *American Builder's Companion*, 6th ed., v–vi.

81. *The Practical House Carpenter* (Boston: R. P. and C. Williams, and Ammin and Smith, 1830); *The Practice of Architecture* (Boston: Benjamin, Carter, Hendie, and Company, 1833); *The Builder's Guide* (Boston: Perkins and Marvin, 1839); *The Elements of Architecture* (Boston: B. B. Massey, 1843).

82. I. T. Frary, *Early Houses of Ohio* (Richmond, Va.: Garrett and Massey, 1936), intro.

83. U.S. Department of the Interior, Works Progress Administration, Federal Writers Project of Ohio, *Chillicothe and Ross Counties* (Chillicothe: Ross County Northwest Territory Committee, 1938), 47.

84. The Hawley House was demolished in 1972, but the mantle was preserved and placed in the Jacob Spores House (1854) near Eugene. Jacob Spores House, Coburg, Lane County, Oregon, National Register, NPS, entered 1977.

85. I checked the Lane County Historical Society, the Oregon Historical Society, and the Jackson County Historical Society for copies of pattern books donated by pioneer carpenters. I checked probate records in the Oregon State Archives and Clatsop County for carpenters listed in the 1850 census.

86. Hamlin provides a comprehensive list of nineteenth-century design books in the bibliography of his *Greek Revival Architecture*, 406–8.

87. Minard Lafever, *The Young Builder's General Instructor* (Newark, N.J.: W. Tuttle and Company, 1829); *The Beauties of Modern Architecture* (New York: D. Appleton and Company, 1835; reprint ed. New York: De Capo Press, 1968), v–vi.

88. Minard Lafever, *The Modern Builder's Guide* (New York: Collins and Hanney, 1833), 1–5.

89. Lafever, *Beauties of Modern Architecture*, vii–ix.

90. Lafever and Benjamin differed in that Lafever provided instructions for constructing an entire building, whereas Benjamin concentrated on detailing. The Sam Brown House in Oregon may have been designed using one of Lafever's plates. This house will be discussed in more detail in Chapter 6.

91. Hamlin, *Greek Revival Architecture*, 164–65.

92. Sally McMurry, *Families and Farmhouses in 19th Century America* (New York: Oxford University Press, 1988).

CHAPTER 3

1. Jesse S. Douglas, "Origins of the Population of Oregon, 1850," *Pacific Northwest Historical Review* 41 (April 1950): 95–97.

2. In addition to Douglas's study, Dorothy O. Johansen offers an analysis of land grant applications in her "A Working Hypothesis for the Study of Migrations," *Pacific Historical Review* 36 (February 1967): 4–19. To date, the most comprehensive investigation of Oregon's population is William A. Bowen, *Willamette Valley: Migra-*

tion and Settlement on the Oregon Frontier (Seattle: University of Washington Press, 1978).

3. Douglas, "Origins of Population," 105, 108.

4. This summary of regional Greek Revival house types is drawn from a comparison of several hundred examples of Greek Revival houses in the National Register of Historic Places and the Historic American Building Survey.

5. Shryock's father, Matthias, was a respected carpenter in Kentucky, and he arranged for his son to study for a year with Strickland. The elder Shryock's will indicates that he owned a copy of Asher Benjamin's *Carpenter's Guide*. Clay Lancaster, "Gideon Shryock and John McMurtry: Architect and Builder in Kentucky," *The Art Quarterly* 56 (Autumn 1943): 258.

6. Alfred Andrews, "Gideon Shryock — Kentucky Architect and the Greek Revival Architecture in Kentucky," *The Filson Club Quarterly* 56 (Autumn 1944): 67–77; Andrews, "Greek Revival Architecture in Kentucky" (M.A. thesis, Columbia University, 1944), 27–32.

7. Lancaster, "Gideon Shryock and John McMurtry," 265–72.

8. For the purposes of this study, Missouri is not included with the southern states. Although there were plantation mansions in Missouri, the architecture was generally more like midwestern buildings. Further, nearly all of the emigrants from Missouri were not slave owners. If Missouri were included with the southern states, the South represented 46 percent of Oregon's population in 1850.

9. Quoted in Marcus Whiffen, *American Architecture Since 1780: A Guide to the Styles* (Cambridge, Mass.: MIT Press, 1969), 46.

10. Mary Wingfield Scott, *Houses of Old Richmond* (Richmond, Va.: Valentine Museum, n.d.), 179–81; William Beers House, Richmond (independent city — i.e., no county), Virginia, National Register, NPS, entered 1969.

11. Anderson Barrett House, Richmond, Virginia, National Register, NPS, entered 1972.

12. Without Missouri, the Midwest would constitute 35 percent of Oregon's 1850 population.

13. Frary, *Early Ohio Houses*, 51.

14. Zeno Kent House, Aurora vicinity, Portage County, Ohio, National Register, NPS, entered 1973; Judge Eben Newton House, Canfield, Mahoning County, Ohio, National Register, NPS, entered 1974.

15. Frary, *Early Houses of Ohio*, 125, 130–32. When these houses were studied and photographed by I. T. Frary in 1936, they were about to collapse. Unfortunately, the author was unable to document the dates, original owners, or the builders for these structures. The Ohio State Historic Preservation office cannot confirm whether these houses are still standing.

16. Joshua Giddings Law Office, Jefferson City, Ashtabula County, Ohio, National Historic Landmark, NPS, entered 1974.

17. *Portland, Multnomah County, Oregon* (San Francisco: Kuchel and Dresel, 1858).

18. Ross, "Architecture in Oregon, 1845–1895," 38.

19. Seymour Dunbar, *A History of Travel in America* (New York: Tudor Publishing Company, 1937), 1065–67, 1083, 1109.

20. Sandusky County Courthouse, Fremont, Sandusky County, Ohio, HABS, Library of Congress, 1934.

21. Frary, *Early Houses in Ohio*, 202–07; Painesville City Hall (Old Lake County Courthouse), Painesville, Lake County, Ohio, National Register, NPS, entered 1972; Knox

County Courthouse, Mt. Vernon, Knox County, Ohio, National Register, NPS, entered 1973; Montgomery County Courthouse, Dayton, Montgomery County, Ohio, National Register, NPS, entered 1970.

22. Frary, *Early Houses in Ohio*, 205–7.

23. St. Peter-In-Chains Cathredral, Cincinnati, Hamilton County, Ohio, National Register, NPS, entered 1973.

24. Freewill Baptist Church, Colebrook, Ohio, HABS, Library of Congress, 1937.

25. Bray Hammond, *Banks and Politics in America, From the Revolution to the Civil War* (Princeton, N.J.: Princeton University Press, 1957), 300.

26. Terre Haute Branch of the Second State Bank of Indiana, Terre Haute, Vigo County, Indiana, National Register, NPS, entered 1973.

27. Old State Bank, Vincennes, Knox County, Indiana, National Register, NPS, entered 1974.

28. Many railroad lines in Indiana were constructed on the level banks of the obsolete canal systems. Dunbar, *History of Travel*, 825, 846.

29. Canal House, Connersville, Fayette County, Indiana, National Register, NPS, entered 1973.

30. Old Courthouse, South Bend, St. Joseph County, Indiana, National Register, NPS, entered 1970; Old Courthouse, South Bend, Indiana, HABS, Library of Congress, 1934.

31. The bank cost $80,000 to construct, which was a substantial expenditure for that day. State Bank of Shawneetown, Shawneetown, Gallatin County, Illinois, National Register, NPS, entered 1972.

32. Ibid. Unfortunately, the architect for this structure is unknown.

33. Old State Bank, Shawneetown, Illinois, HABS, Library of Congress, 1934.

34. Galena Historic District, Galena, Jo Daviess County, Illinois, National Register, NPS, entered 1969; Chicago Portage National Historic Site, Forest View, Cook County, Illinois, National Historic Landmark, NPS, entered 1966.

35. Fred Gross, the local surveyor for HABS, researched the Henderson County records and discovered an Abner Hebbard listed as a local architect in 1842. Gross could not associate the designer directly with the courthouse, but he suggests Hebbard as a logical source for the plans. Henderson County Courthouse, Oquawka, Illinois, HABS, Library of Congress, 1936. The bricks were coated with plaster in 1905. The surveyor obtained his information from Charles Shell, a local blacksmith who had observed the changes to the courthouse from about 1860 until the 1930s. Ibid.

36. Joseph Hoge House, Galena, Illinois, HABS, Library of Congress, 1934. Galena Historic District, National Register, 1969.

37. Telford House, Galena, Illinois, HABS, Library of Congress, 1934.

38. Swartout House, Waukegan, Illinois, HABS, Library of Congress, 1934.

39. The data sheet for the Newton Farmhouse has been misplaced by the Library of Congress. Without this information, it is necessary to study the house on its architectural merits alone. As far as I can determine, the house is not recorded in any other surveys.

40. Newton Farmhouse, Belvidere, Illinois, HABS, Library of Congress, n.d.

41. The Newton Farmhouse bears a striking resemblance to the Jacob Spores House near Eugene, Oregon, in plan, scale, and detailing. In fact, the entrances through the extensions on both houses are nearly identical. Spores House, National Register, 1977.

42. William B. Sappington House, Arrow Rock vicinity, Saline County, Missouri, National Register, NPS, entered 1970.

43. The data sheet for the Aull House has been misplaced by the Library of Congress. The only surviving evidence is a photograph and the approximate date of 1845.

44. John C. Ainsworth House, Oregon City, Clackamas County, Oregon, National Register, entered 1973.

45. George L. Caley, *Footprints of the Past* (Smyrna, Del.: Shane Quality Press, 1978), 151–52; Woodlawn (Thomas England House), Smyrna vicinity, Kent County, Delaware, National Register, NPS, entered 1982.

46. "Preservation and Development Plan for the Sam Houston Memorial Museum," prepared by Bell, Klein, and Hoffman, Architects and Restoration Consultants for Sam Houston State University (October 1975), 22–25.

47. Woodland (Sam Houston House), Huntsville, Walker County, Texas, National Historic Landmark, NPS, entered 1966.

48. The Donation Land Claim was authorized by an act of Congress on 29 September 1850. It granted all male settlers over the age of eighteen 320 acres of land if they had occupied and cultivated the land for at least four years before 1850. For those — like Colver — who settled in Oregon after 1850, they were entitled to 160 acres if they were at least twenty-one years old. Also, their wives could claim 160 acres. An amendment in 1853 required claimants to pay $1.25 an acre. Johansen and Gates, *Empire of the Columbia*, 231.

49. "Colver House Receives Marker," *Table Rock Sentinel, Newsletter of the Southern Oregon Historical Society* 1 (March 1981): 4; Sonja Swinney, "The House of Many Faces [Samuel Colver House]" (Unpublished research paper, Southern Oregon Historical Society, Jacksonville, 1960).

50. The date Colver added siding and the portico to his house has not been recorded. Judging from the dates of the other classical houses in the area, however, it was the late 1850s or early 1860s.

CHAPTER 4

1. Alvin T. Smith Diary, 13 February–23 March 1840.

2. The Smiths and the other members of their party were independent missionaries to Oregon. Unlike most missionaries in the Pacific Northwest at that time, they were not affiliated with or receiving funds from any denomination or religious organization.

3. Smith and his party traveled to the Whitman Mission by way of the mission cutoff, which turned north toward present-day Walla Walla, Washington, after crossing the Blue Mountains. This route was the typical path for most immigrants in the early 1840s, but by about 1845 most of the pioneers went overland from the Blue Mountains in a direct line of travel to The Dalles, Oregon.

4. The Smiths had just spent a week helping the Griffins through marital difficulties, and the journey was perhaps an example of 1840s family therapy. Smith Diary, 13–28 September 1840.

5. Quoted in Clifford Drury, *Marcus and Narcissa Whitman and the Opening of Old Oregon*, 2 vols. (Glendale, Calif.: Arthur H. Clark Company, 1973), 2:384. Green earlier had cautioned the Whitmans and Spaldings to dissociate themselves from independent missionaries. Spalding was demonstrating here that at least some independents were valuable assets to mission work.

6. Smith Diary, 22, 28, 30 September 1841. The Reverend Alvin Waller and former mountain man Robert Newell assisted Smith in locating a settlement site near the Tualatin group of the Kalapuya Indians.

7. Ibid., 14, 18–30 October 1841; William A. Bowen, *Willamette Valley*, 73–75.

8. Bowen, *Willamette Valley*, 73. Bowen hypothesizes that Smith and other early pioneers used mortise and tenon joint construction and bound the entire structure with hazel switches in place of ropes or wires. This theory is plausible, since Smith does not mention any nails or other hardware in his description.

9. Smith Diary, March–June 1842, passim.

10. The "post-in-the-sill" construction technique survives today in the original granary at reconstructed Fort Nisqually, Point Defiance Park, Tacoma, Washington, and in St. Paul's Mission near Colville, Washington. John Hussey, *A History of Fort Vancouver and Its Physical Plan* (Tacoma: Washington State Historical Society, 1957), passim; Vaughan and Ferriday, eds., *Space Style and Structure*, 1:36–37.

11. Forts Boise, Hall, and Walla Walla were constructed with adobe. None of these structures survive. Vaughan and Ferriday, eds., *Space and Style and Structure*, 1:38–39.

12. Ibid., 39–40; Jason Lee House, Salem, Marion County, Oregon, National Register nomination, NPS, entered 1973.

13. Quoted in Vaughan and Ferriday, eds., *Space, Style, and Structure*, 1:81–82.

14. John Minto, "Reminiscences of Experiences on the Oregon Trail in 1844," *Oregon Historical Quarterly* 2 (September 1901): 232, hereafter cited as *OHQ*.

15. Philip Foster Papers, MSS 996, Manuscript Library, Oregon Historical Society, Portland, Oregon. Daily record books for this partnership survive for the years 1843 and 1844.

16. Philip Dole has studied buildings in Oregon for many years by looking at the available documentation and making physical inspections. He has observed that most pioneer families built simple shelters when they first arrived in Oregon. Within a period of months or years they constructed hewn-log houses, and finally more permanent lumber dwellings. He also notes that "barns are always built before the house." Vaughan and Ferriday, eds., *Space, Style and Structure*, 1:83, 243–44.

17. David N. Birdseye House, Rogue River vicinity, Jackson County, Oregon, National Register nomination, NPS, entered 1974; *Medford* (Oregon) *Mail Tribune*, 4 January 1980. The Birdseye House is currently undergoing major restoration.

18. Horace Baker Cabin, Carver vicinity, Clackamas County, Oregon, National Register nomination, NPS, entered 1976.

19. John Stauffer House and Barn, Hubbard vicinity, Marion County, Oregon, National Register nomination, NPS, entered 1974; Vaughan and Ferriday, eds., *Space, Style, and Structure*, 1:148–49.

20. John Minto describes a simple barn he and his associates built for Morton M. McCarver in 1844. They cut the logs and assembled the structure in two days. Minto, "Reminiscences," 231.

21. H. S. Nedry, ed., "Willamette Valley in 1859: The Diary of a Tour," *OHQ* 46 (September 1945): 243–44.

22. Smith Diary, January 1843–February 1844, passim.

23. Marion Ross, "Architecture in Oregon, 1845–1895," 37; Dr. John McLoughlin House, Oregon City, Clackamas County, Oregon, HABS, Library of Congress, 1934.

Notes

24. The Ermatinger House was "discovered" in 1976 after a period of about fifty years when nobody remembered where the house was located or even if it was still standing. It had been moved from its original location during the early 1900s and remodeled to the point that it no longer looked historic. A local historian identified the house when he crawled into the attic and noticed the earlier, distinctive flat roof. Francis Ermatinger House, Oregon City, Clackamas County, Oregon, National Register nomination, NPS, entered 1977.

25. Dr. Forbes Barclay House, Oregon City, Clackamas County, Oregon, National Register nomination, NPS, entered 1974.

26. *Oregon City* (Oregon) *Spectator*, 7, 16, 24 August 1848.

27. Ibid., 17 October 1848. Indeed the editor was correct, for in the early 1850s gold was discovered at Jacksonville, Oregon, and Gold Beach on the Oregon Coast. Then in the 1860s, there were new strikes in eastern Oregon.

28. Rodman W. Paul, *Mining Frontiers of the Far West, 1848–1880* (New York: Holt, Rinehart, and Winston, 1963), 15.

29. Eva Emery Dye, "Women's Part in the Drama of the Northwest," *Oregon Pioneer Association Transactions* 21 (1894): 43, hereafter cited as *OPAT*.

30. John Minto, "Robert Wilson Morrison," *OPAT* 21 (1894): 61.

31. Alvin T. Smith noted in his diary on 7 September 1848 that the mother of Calvin B. Green arranged for the Smiths to care for her son. She would either pay them when she returned from California, or if she did not come back, "She wished us to keep him as our son." Four days later Smith says that Joseph Gale sent his children, Edward and Susan, to stay with them until he returned from the goldfields. Gale sent $250 a year to Smith for the care of his children. Smith Diary, 7, 11 September 1848. According to the Oregon Census of 1850, Susan Gale and three of her sisters were staying with the Smiths, but her brother and the Green boy were not. U.S. Census Office, *Seventh Census of the United States, 1850*, Oregon Schedule (Washington: J. D. B. De Bow, 1854), hereafter cited as Oregon Census, 1850.

32. Abigail Smith to Jane Gray Ogden, 24 February 1853, Alvin T. Smith Collection, Oregon Historical Society.

33. Burnett and his partners were more successful than many of their fellow miners because they carried all of their necessities, food, picks, shovels, clothing, and the materials for a sluice box in their wagons. Burnett later recalled that the only item he purchased in California was a jar of molasses. Peter H. Burnett, "Recollections and Opinions of an Old Pioneer," *OHQ* 5 (December 1904): 272–305.

34. *Oregon City* (Oregon) *Spectator*, 17 October 1848.

35. Smith Diary, 6 May 1847.

36. These figures are taken from the Smith Diary for the years 1847–48.

37. Ibid., 1850; *Oregon City* (Oregon) *Spectator*, 30 May and 27 June 1850.

38. Arthur L. Throckmorton, *Oregon Argonauts: Merchant Adventurers on the Western Frontier* (Portland: Oregon Historical Society, 1961), 93.

39. Ibid., 88–102.

40. Mrs. W. W. Buck, "Reminiscences," *OPAT* 21 (1891): 69.

41. Smith Diary, 1848–51.

42. Hubert Howe Bancroft, *The History of Oregon*, 2 vols. (San Francisco: History Company, 1888), 2:58–61.

43. Harriet K. McArthur, "A Biographical Sketch of Hon. J. W. Nesmith," *OPAT* 13 (1886): 31–32; James W. Nesmith House, Rickreall, Marion County, Oregon, HABS, Library of Congress, 1934. When this house was recorded for HABS in 1934, much

Notes

of the Greek Revival detailing was intact. During the 1950s, the house was completely remodeled and is no longer distinguishable as a classical structure.

44. Jacob Spores House, Coburg vicinity, Lane County, Oregon, National Register
nomination, NPS, entered 1977.

45. *Oregon City* (Oregon) *Spectator*, 18 April 1850.

46. The Spores House will be discussed in more detail in the next chapter.

47. The owner, a Mr. Stokes, went to the goldfields and sold 320 acres to Peter Hatch, a
deacon in the Oregon City Congregational Church. Hatch thought he had acquired
the other half section from Stokes while he was in California and sold this land to
the Walkers. When Stokes returned to Forest Grove in 1851, he was completely
broke and demanded the return of his property. For whatever reason, the issue was
decided by the Congregational Church of Forest Grove, and the land was returned
to Stokes. There is no evidence to suggest that the Walkers received any cash
settlement from their lost land. Clifford Drury, ed., *Nine Years with the Spokane
Indians: The Diary, 1838–1848, of Elkanah Walker* (Glendale, Calif.: Arthur H. Clark
Company, 1976), 491, 493–94.

48. Myron Eells, "Mrs. Mary Richardson Walker," *OPAT* 24 (1897): 140.

49. John D. Unruh, Jr., *The Plains Across: The Overland Emigrants and the Trans-Mississippi West, 1840–1860* (Urbana: University of Illinois Press, 1979), 119–20.

50. Quoted in Dorothy O. Johansen, "A Working Hypothesis," 8. To outsiders this
story appears to be fictitious, but to native Oregonians it is still the gospel truth.

51. Some of these newcomers who immigrated to Oregon by way of California built
Greek Revival houses. They and their houses will be discussed in more detail in the
next chapter.

52. William Sperry was my great-great-grandfather, and the three-week-old baby,
Samantha Alice, was my great-grandmother.

53. Mark V. Weatherford, *The Sperry-Weatherford Family* (Albany, Oreg.: n.p., 1960),
3–16.

54. Southwest of the present-day city of Oroville, California, there is a small community called Oregon House. Nearby, a California state marker commemorates the
mining camp called Oregon City, where Peter Burnett and his associates staked
their claims.

55. Bancroft, *History of Oregon*, 1:46.

56. Ibid., 46–47.

57. *Oregon City* (Oregon) *Spectator*, 8 February 1849.

58. Donald McLeod to Alvin T. Smith, 4 July 1849, Smith Collection, Oregon Historical
Society.

59. H. S. Lyman, "Reminiscences of Hugh Cosgrove," *OHQ* 1 (June 1900): 246–66.

60. "James Duval Holman," *OPAT* 21 (1894): 45.

61. Reprinted in *OPAT* 15 (1888): 52.

62. Bowen, *Willamette Valley*, 100–101.

63. Mrs. Buck recalled that the building site she and her husband purchased in Oregon
City cost $3,000. This figure was common for that time and was probably the price
Barclay paid for his house lot. Therefore, Meek's statistics in this case were correct.
Meek's estimates ranged from $3,000 to $25,000 in Oregon City. These figures
match those in other accounts and are, therefore, generally reliable.

64. Thirty-two houses have been recorded in the Historic American Building Survey,
the National Register of Historic Places, or the Statewide Inventory of Historic Sites

and Buildings. For six structures, photographs are the only surviving documentation, without any names or locations for these dwellings. These photographs are included in the Jameson Parker Collection at the Oregon Historical Society, and they do not have any identification names or numbers. Reliable information for the remaining twenty-six owners means either that they are included in the 1850 or 1860 censuses, or that biographical data are available in the *OPAT*, newspapers, or letters from the family, or some combination of the above.

65. Of the twenty-three owners who lived in the Midwest, four lived in at least three states, seven in two states, and the rest in one state. In the last category, several of these owners may have lived in more midwestern states, but their biographical or census records do not indicate it.

66. Douglas, "Origins of Population," 110.

67. Johansen, "A Working Hypothesis," 4.

68. Bowen, *Willamette Valley*, 95.

69. This figure is based on the 3,404 adult males identified by Douglas in his article. Douglas, "Origins of Population," 110.

70. My analysis of the 1860 census records was not as detailed as the work already done on the 1850 census. The procedure was to spot check the 1860 entries to locate the names and occupations of these men. Eleven "carpenters" were listed among several occupations, but the others may have been in the state as late as 1859 still practicing as carpenters.

71. The *Oregon City* (Oregon) *Spectator* and the documentation for the Barclay House demonstrate that carpenters made as much as ten dollars per day during the gold rush, and building laborers made four to six dollars a day. With these wages, the building industry was a desirable occupation in 1850. Case and Philips will be discussed in greater detail in the next chapter. In addition to these men, Philip Foster and Jacob Wain, the building contractors described earlier in this chapter, also were listed as farmers in 1850.

72. Among this group twenty-one men were single, but they were over twenty-five years old. Most of these carpenters owned property and were included in the 1860 census. At least some of these builders probably lived in other midwestern states before they came to Oregon.

73. All these thirty-one men lived in the Midwest for less than ten years, or for periods of time that cannot be determined from the census. Many undoubtedly saw classical architecture in that region before they came to Oregon. Fourteen of the remaining carpenters were single men over the age of twenty-five who owned property in 1850. Some of these builders probably lived in one or more middle states before venturing to the West.

74. Bowen found that 54 percent of Oregon's 1850 population (adults and children) came from the Midwest. Douglas determined that 59 percent (adult and children) came from that region. Bowen, *Willamette Valley*, 25; Douglas, "Origins of Population," 110. Johansen's figures were based solely on marriage data from land records. Johansen, "A Working Hypothesis," 4.

75. The Kuckel and Dresel lithograph for Portland, printed in 1858, indicates that several small classical revival buildings were standing in Portland at that time. Although Greek Revival houses perhaps were present as well, these were not recorded before they were demolished.

76. Smith Diary, 31 December 1850, and entries for the year of 1850.

Notes

CHAPTER 5

1. Smith Diary, 1851–53.

2. Tualatin Academy (Old College Hall), Pacific University campus, Forest Grove, Washington County, Oregon, National Register, NPS, entered 1974.

3. When Smith obtained the help of neighbors or hired workers on other projects, he usually referred to their assistance in his diary. He did not mention the aid of others in the construction of his new house. Smith Diary, passim.

4. Ibid., 1 November 1854. While the lean-to appears as a later addition to the house, the detailing is identical to and therefore contemporary with the main portion of the structure. Alvin T. Smith House, Forest Grove vicinity, Washington County, Oregon, National Register, NPS, entered 1974. Smith's diary shows that the lean-to was part of the original structure. He later referred to the addition as a storage shed. Ibid., 18 December 1857.

5. Whitlow was not included in the 1850 Oregon census, and the 1860 census showed that he had moved to Benton County.

6. Smith Diary, 6 November 1854, 18 September, 8, 14 November, and 13 December 1855.

7. Please refer to Chapters 1 and 3.

8. Smith House nomination. There are a number of architectural surveys for Connecticut. In these, the templelike format is predominant for Greek Revival houses. In addition to the nominations for Branford (Smith's hometown), the Coit houses (also referred to as "Whale Oil Row") in New London, the Samuel Russell House in Middletown, 19 S. Main Street in Colchester, and the Major Timothy Cowles House in Farmington are examples from different areas of the state. "Opportunities for Historic Preservation: Southeastern Connecticut Region," November 1968. Southeastern Connecticut Regional Planning Agency, Norwich; "Connecticut Houses."

9. The William Case entry in the 1850 Oregon census provides an interesting example of the discrepancies between biographical and census data. According to his biographies, he was born in Indiana, but the census indicates that he was born in either Louisiana or Virginia. The handwriting in his entry for 1850 is unclear — the first letter either is a V or an L. This particular census taker did not record other individuals from Louisiana, and the Vs for Virginia are different.

10. Lyman, "Reminiscences of William M. Case," *OHQ* 1 (September 1900): 271–77, 290; "William Case, 1820–1903, Champoeg, Oregon," typed manuscript, n.d., in the William M. Case House, National Register nomination file, Oregon State Parks and Recreation Division, Department of Transportation, Salem, hereafter cited as Oregon State Parks.

11. Vaughan and Ferriday, eds., *Space, Style, and Structure*, 1:116; William M. Case House, Champoeg vicinity, Marion County, Oregon, National Register, NPS, entered 1973.

12. The Prudhomme House, built in about 1800, is one of the oldest surviving Creole plantation houses in northern Louisiana. The floor plan, overall dimensions, open gallery, and roof pitch are remarkably similar to the Case House. Some of the variations, such as the sleeping porches, the outside doorways to many of the rooms, and the frame and mud plaster construction of the Louisiana example can be attributed to the climatic and geographical differences. Narcisse Prudhomme Plantation (Beau Fort), Bermuda, Natchitoches Parish, Louisiana, National Register, NPS, entered 1976. Professor Dole contends that Case derived the plan for his house from retired French-Canadian trappers who settled near Champoeg. While this theory seems logical, Dole does not explain the differences between French

188

Notes

influences from Quebec and those from Louisiana. Vaughan and Ferriday, eds., *Space, Style, and Structure,* 1:116.

13. Ibid., 1:131–33; Case House nomination.

14. Randall V. Mills, *Stern-Wheelers Up Columbia: A Century of Steamboating in the Oregon Country* (Palo Alto, Calif.: Pacific Books, 1947; reprint ed., Lincoln: University of Nebraska Press, 1977), 19–21.

15. Bancroft, *History of Oregon,* 1:480; Dorothy O. Johansen, "Oregon Steam Navigation Company: An Example of Capitalism on the Frontier," *Pacific Historical Review* 10 (June 1941): 179–81, 184–85, 188.

16. The bank he established was the predecessor for the United States National Bank of Oregon, one of the largest financial institutions in the state. Harvey W. Scott, *History of the Oregon Country,* 2 vols. (Cambridge, Mass.: Riverside Press, 1924), 2:273–74.

17. John C. Ainsworth autobiography. Original in Oregon Historical Society Manuscript Library. Copy used was a microfilm version from the Huntington Library.

18. These data come from the 1850 manuscript census for Oregon.

19. A former owner, Mrs. Albert H. Powers, suggested that the tight layout of interior rooms made the Ainsworth House uncomfortable. She studied the chain of title and discovered that most of the owners lived in the house for only a short period of time. Captain Ainsworth himself sold the house and moved to Portland within a short period to manage the Oregon Steam Navigation Company. Interview with Mrs. Albert H. Powers, 16 January 1977.

20. Captain John C. Ainsworth House, Oregon City vicinity, Clackamas County, Oregon, National Register, NPS, entered 1973.

21. Hugh Fields House, Brownsville vicinity, Linn County, Oregon, National Register, NPS, entered 1989.

22. Elizabeth Esson Brown, "History of the Brown House," *Marion County History* 1 (1955): 6.

23. Sam Brown (the carpenter) did not appear in the 1850 census.

24. Frederick Doveton Nichols, *Thomas Jefferson's Architectural Drawings* (Boston: Massachusetts Historical Society, 1961), 11; Pierson, *American Buildings,* 292–93; Federal Hill, Forest vicinity, Campbell County, Virginia, National Register, NPS, entered 1982; Lafever, *Beauties of Modern Architecture,* 42. A number of other examples of this house plan can be seen in Massachusetts, New York, Connecticut, Vermont, and Maine.

25. The paint texture technique was common in areas where marble was unavailable or very expensive. In some areas such as Little Rock, Arkansas, craftsmen perfected the process to a degree that an untrained eye cannot readily detect the difference between stone and the artificial treatment. Old Arkansas Capitol nomination, entered 1969.

26. During the winter, passengers often stayed overnight on the journey from Portland to Salem. In the summer, the stage lines usually made the trip in one day. Brown, "History of the Brown House," 7.

27. Many Oregon houses of the same period used the box construction framing system. With this method, vertical boards were connected to the sill beams at the bottom and a hewn timber beam on the top. The attachment of horizontal weather boards on the outside provided a durable frame. While many of the houses constructed with this system have survived for 130 years or longer, the beam framing

method, such as that used on the Brown House, was usually superior. Vaughan and Ferriday, eds., *Space, Style, and Structure*, 1: 98–99.

28. In 1940 the Browns were awarded a prize at the Oregon State Fair by a cedar shingle company for the most durable shingles in the state. Brown, "History of the Brown House," 6.

29. Interview with Sam Brown III, Gervais, Oregon, 26 January 1977; Sam Brown House, Gervais vicinity, Marion County, Oregon, National Register, NPS, entered 1974.

30. Thomas Vaughan, *The Bybee-Howell House on Sauvie Island* (Portland: Oregon Historical Society, 1974), 2–7.

31. Johansen, "A Working Hypothesis," 10.

32. Sheila Ann Finch wrote a master's thesis on the Bybee houses in 1970. She thoroughly studied the architecture of both dwellings and devoted much of her attention to the similarities. She concluded that William did not see James's house and vice versa, but the idea for both structures probably came from a house type in Kentucky, familiar to both men. Sheila Ann Finch, "The Bybee Houses and the Appearance of the Greek Revival in Oregon" (M.A. thesis, University of Oregon, 1970), 22–41.

33. Most Oregon houses through the 1870s had plaster walls and painted ceilings but not the elaborate plaster moldings found in the both Bybee houses. Vaughan and Ferriday, eds., *Space, Style, and Structure*, 1:105.

34. Bybee-Howell House, Sauvie Island, Multnomah County, Oregon, National Register, NPS, entered 1974.

35. A family tradition suggests that Bybee actually lost his house in a horse race in Montana. Don Bybee to the Southern Oregon Historical Society, 16 August 1982; Larry McGraw, a Portland fireman and amateur pomologist, developed an orchard on the property with historical varieties of fruit trees gathered from around the United States in the early 1970s.

36. *Grants Pass* (Oregon) *Rogue River Courier*, 28 April 1905; *Medford* (Oregon) *Mail Tribune*, 12 November 1908; "William Bybee: Land Baron," *Table Rock Sentinel: Newsletter of the Southern Oregon Historical Society* 1 (July 1981): 3–5.

37. William M. Bybee House, Jacksonville vicinity, Jackson County, Oregon, National Register, NPS, entered 1977.

38. The 1850 census notes that the oldest Spores child born in Illinois was fourteen years old when the family left for Oregon, indicating that Jacob lived in Illinois for a minimum of fourteen years.

39. A drawing in A. G. Walling, *An Illustrated History of Lane County, Oregon* (Portland: Western Publishing Company, 1884), 108, shows the house and barn in their original setting. A Mr. Williamson, a railroad surveyor, spent the night in the Spores House on 4 October 1855. This reference places the construction date at some time before 1855. Spores House nomination.

40. Newton House data, Chapter 4; Spores House nomination.

41. Interviews with Gregg A. Olsen, July–October 1975 and March 1977. Also, he noted that some of the detail work on the Case and Ainsworth houses required talented craftsmen and specialized equipment.

42. Double house is the term used for structures that are unusually long and narrow with equal living space on each side of a central wall. In many of these structures, a double fireplace was located on both sides to provide efficient heating for the entire house. During the 1800s there were several double houses in the Willamette Valley. Of the remaining structures, the Spores House and the Charles Applegate

House near Yoncalla in Douglas County are perhaps the best examples. Philip Dole, "Farmhouses and Barns in Early Lane County," *Lane County Historian* 10 (August 1965): 28–31. The ell was reconstructed during the recent restoration. A new section was added onto the rear of the original ell to accommodate an extra bedroom and a modern kitchen. Interview with Gregg A. Olsen, 16 March 1978; Spores House nomination.

43. Benjamin, *The Builder's Guide*, Plate 52.

44. As historian for the Oregon State Historic Preservation Office, I was one of the staff members who looked at the Andrew Smith House. This site inspection and the subsequent research necessary to prepare the National Register nomination form became a major stimulus for the present study.

45. Joel Palmer, "Diaries of Joel Palmer" (1860), typescript manuscript, Oregon State Library, Salem.

46. Sarah Smith to Andrew Smith, 6 March 1860, Andrew Smith Folder, MSS 86, Manuscript Collection, Oregon Historical Society, Portland, Oregon.

47. Although the builder of the Smith House is unknown, a local historian uncovered the account book of a Mr. Chaplin, a fashion door and sash maker in Dayton. Chaplin's name did not appear in the 1850 census, but it was included in 1860. The account book showed that Chaplin started his business in 1858, that his shop was destroyed in a flood in 1860, and that after the flood, he moved to eastern Oregon. Thus Chaplin owned the proper equipment to construct intricate moldings and may have been the carpenter for the Smith House. Interview with Ruth Stoller, Dayton, Oregon, 9 May 1975.

48. Andrew Smith House, Dayton, Yamhill County, Oregon, National Register nomination, NPS, entered 1976.

49. Memorandum to the files, 20 April 1973, Darius B. Cartwright file, Oregon State Parks, Salem.

50. Information sheet provided to HABS by Mary Stevens, Eugene, Oregon, in 1933. Jameson Parker Collection, Oregon Historical Society.

51. *Genealogical Material in Oregon Donation Land Claims Abstracted from Applications*, 3 vols. (Portland: Genealogical Forum of Portland, 1962), 3:37.

52. Granville H. Baber House, Albany vicinity, Linn County, Oregon, National Register, NPS, entered 1975.

53. Baber House nomination; Granville H. Baber House, data sheet (HABS ORE–32), Jameson Parker Collection, Oregon Historical Society; H. O. Lang, ed., *History of the Willamette Valley* (Portland: Hines and Lang, 1885), 631; Katherine Harris, "Pioneer Knox Butte House Still Used After 108 Years," *Salem* (Oregon) *Capitol Journal*, 8 February 1954. This author placed the date of construction at 1846, which is the year Baber filed for a provisional government land claim. Using other classical houses for reference, this date was too early, but the article is valuable for its biographical information on Baber.

54. A geometric pattern for fluted and tapered columns similar to those used in the Baber House was available in Asher Benjamin's *American Builder's Companion*, 6th ed., Plate 7.

55. H. K. Hines, *An Illustrated History of the State of Oregon* (Chicago: Lewis Publishing Co., 1893), 848–49.

56. Several examples are extant or recorded in New Orleans. A house (now demolished) that was located on Magazine Street and built during the 1830s is nearly identical to the Phillips House in configuration and detailing. Another similar house is located at 1536 Chippewa Street. Other examples are located at 1905–1907 Burgundy (ca. 1830), 2014 Ursulines (ca. 1835), and 927 N. Galvez (1837). Mary

Louise Christovich et al., eds., *New Orleans Architecture*, 6 vols. — vol. 1: *The Lower Garden District, Howard Avenue to Jackson Avenue, Mississippi River to Claiborne Avenue*, vol. 4: *The Creole Faubourgs*, vol. 6: *Faubourg Tremé and the Bayou Road, North Rampart Street to North Broad Street, Canal Street to St. Bernard Avenue* (Gretna, La.: Pelican Publishing Company, 1974–80), 1:41, 4:102, 6:46.

57. John Phillips House, Salem vicinity, Polk County, Oregon, National Register, NPS, entered 1976.

58. A "saddlebag" house is a variation of the "double house" described earlier in the Spores House notation. Generally, these dwellings were constructed with two or four cubic "pens" or rooms on either side of the breezeway. The living quarters and open hallway were covered with a simple gabled roof. Other common terms for these dwellings were "double pen" or "dogtrot" houses. The latter was the preferred term, and it meant that a four-legged "critter" was permitted to "trot" through the breezeway. The expression also implied that in the hot southern climate, cool air could more easily pass through the opening and circulate through the entire dwelling. Kniffen, "Louisiana House Types," 179–93.

59. Edward Shaw, *Rural Architecture* (Boston: James B. Dow, 1843), Plates 13 and 14. Shaw's work was popular during the 1840s and 1850s, and his principal stylistic mode was classical revival. Ross, "Architecture in Oregon, 1845–1895," 38–39.

60. Jacob Conser House, Jefferson, Marion County, Oregon, National Register, NPS, entered 1974.

61. Leroy and Ann W. Hafen, eds., *To the Rockies and Oregon, 1839–1842*, 3 vols. (Glendale, Calif.: Arthur H. Clark Company, 1955), 3:135.

62. In recent years, the Cook House has been remodeled, damaging much of the classical detailing. Fortunately, HABS recorded the structure in 1934 before the work was done. These photographs and drawings provide substantial information on the original appearance of the house. Amos Cook file (HABS ORE–32), Manuscript Collection, Oregon Historical Society, Portland; letter from Agnes C. Bradshaw (daughter of Amos Cook) to Jameson Parker, 7 February 1934, Jameson Parker Collection, Oregon Historical Society; Amos Cook House, Dayton vicinity, Yamhill County, Oregon, National Register, NPS, entered 1974.

63. The existing front porch on the Fletcher House is somewhat confusing. The four Doric columns give the house a Greek Revival appearance. Yet the porch and pillars were added in the 1920s to replace an earlier structure. Francis Fletcher House, Dayton vicinity, Yamhill County, Oregon, National Register, NPS, entered 1975.

64. Vaughan and Ferriday, eds., *Space, Style, and Structure*, 1:118–20.

65. Restoration files on the Wolf Creek Tavern, 1977–1978, Oregon State Parks; interview with Gregg A. Olsen, member of the research team, May 1990.

66. Wolf Creek Tavern, Wolf Creek, Josephine County, Oregon, National Register, NPS, entered 1972.

67. Thomas Vaughan and George McMath, *A Century of Portland Architecture* (Portland: Oregon Historical Society, 1967), 17–20; Terrence O'Donnell and Thomas Vaughan, *Portland: A Historical Sketch and Guide* (Portland: Oregon Historical Society, 1976), 76–77.

68. Waller Hall is nearly identical to another academic structure completed in Philomath, near Corvallis, the same year. Philomath Academy was an institution of the United Brethren Church, which began with the construction of the new building. The remarkable similarity between Waller Hall and Philomath Academy suggests that the same person prepared the plans for both structures. Philomath Academy was always a small college and was finally closed in 1929 due to a low

enrollment and inadequate funding. The academy building is now the Benton County Historical Museum, and except for the extension of the east and west wings, it looks much as it did in 1867. Philomath College, Philomath, Benton County, Oregon, National Register, NPS, entered 1972.

69. Gustavus Hines, *Oregon and Its Institutions* (New York: Carlton and Porter, 1868), 266–67.

70. Waller Hall, Willamette University, Salem, Marion County, Oregon, National Register, NPS, entered 1975.

CHAPTER 6

1. Smith Diary, 1866–68.

2. Historians of Oregon's pioneer heritage generally agree that the settlers were conservative. Gordon B. Dodds, *Oregon: A Bicentennial History* (New York: W. W. Norton and Company, 1977); Johansen and Gates, *Empire of the Columbia*; Earl Pomeroy, *The Pacific Slope: A History of California, Oregon, Washington, Idaho, Utah, and Nevada* (New York: Alfred A. Knopf, 1965); David S. Lavender, *Land of Giants: The Drive in the Pacific Northwest, 1750–1950* (Garden City, N.Y.: Doubleday, 1958).

3. Andrew Jackson Downing, *The Architecture of Country Houses* (New York: D. Appleton and Company, 1856; reprint ed. New York: Dover Publications, Inc., 1969), 82–93. The Surgeon's Quarters looks very much like Design III in Downing's book for a Symmetrical Bracketed Cottage. It is illustrated in Figure 13.

BIBLIOGRAPHY

MANUSCRIPTS

New Haven, Connecticut. Beinecke Rare Book and Manuscript Library. Yale University. Alvin T. Smith Collection. MSS (Sm 5, Sm 515).

New York, New York. Avery Architecture Library. Columbia University. General MSS Collection.

Philadelphia, Pennsylvania. "Historic Structures Report on the Second Bank of the United States." 2 June 1962. Archives. Independence National Historical Park.

Portland, Oregon. Oregon Historical Society. Alvin T. Smith Collection. MSS 8.

———. Andrew Smith Folder. MSS 86.

———. Jameson Parker Collection. MSS 3000.

———. Philip Foster Collection. MSS 996.

San Marino, California. The Huntington Library. Captain John C. Ainsworth Autobiography. Microfilm Collection.

Washington, D.C. Historic American Building Survey. Maps and Photographs Division. Library of Congress.

———. National Register of Historic Places. U.S. Department of the Interior. National Park Service.

GOVERNMENT DOCUMENTS

Connecticut. Connecticut State Library. Bulletin #17. "Connecticut Houses." Compiled by the Connecticut Society of Colonial Dames of America. 1942.

Oregon. Territorial Legislative Assembly. *Report of the Commissioners Appointed to Superintend the Erection of Public Buildings at the Seat of Government.* 5th Sess. 22 December 1853.

"Preservation and Development Plan for the Sam Houston Memorial Museum." Prepared by Bell, Klein, and Hoffman, Architects and Restoration Consultants for Sam Houston State University. October 1975.

Richardson, James D., ed. *A Compilation of the Messages and Papers of the Presidents, 1789–1897.* 12 vols. Washington, D. C.: Government Printing Office, 1898.

Southeastern Connecticut Regional Planning Agency. Norwich. "Opportunities for Historic Preservation: Southeastern Connecticut Region." November 1968.

195

Bibliography

U.S. Census Office. *Seventh Census of the United States, 1850.*
Oregon Schedule. Washington, D.C.: J. D. B. DeBow, 1854.

U.S. Congress. House. *Documentary History of the Construction and Development of the United States Capitol Building and Grounds.* House Report 646. 58th Cong. 2d Sess. 1904.

Vermont. *Journals of the House of Representatives.* 21st Sess. 1833.

INTERVIEWS

Brown, Sam, III. Gervais, Oregon. 26 January 1977.

Olsen, Gregg A. Eugene, Oregon. July–October 1975, March 1977, March 1978, May 1990.

Powers, Mrs. Albert H. Oregon City, Oregon. 16 January 1977.

Stoller, Ruth. Dayton, Oregon. 9 May 1975.

THESES AND DISSERTATIONS

Andrews, Alfred J. "Greek Revival Houses in Kentucky." M.A. thesis, Columbia University, 1944.

Barber, Joel C. "History of the Old State Capitol Buildings of the State of Oregon." M.A. thesis, University of Oregon, 1966.

Cline, Myrtle A. "American Attitude Toward the Greek War of Independence, 1821–1828." Ph.D. dissertation, Columbia University, 1930.

Finch, Sheila Ann. "The Bybee Houses and the Appearance of the Greek Revival in Oregon." M.A. thesis, University of Oregon, 1970.

Norton, Paul F. "Latrobe, Jefferson and the National Capitol." Ph.D. dissertation, Princeton University, 1952.

NEWSPAPERS

Grants Pass (Oregon) *Rogue River Courier.* 28 April 1905.

Medford (Oregon) *Mail Tribune.* 12 November 1908, 4 January 1980.

Oregon City (Oregon) *Spectator.* 7, 16, 24 August, 17 October 1848, 8 February 1849, 18 April, 30 May, and 27 June 1850.

Philadelphia Gazette and Daily Advertiser. 12 May 1818.

Salem (Oregon) *Capital Journal.* 8 February 1954.

Salem (Oregon) *Statesman.* 12 December 1854, 18 December 1855, 29 January 1856.

Bibliography

ARTICLES

Ames, Kenneth. "Robert Mills and the Philadelphia Row House." *Journal of the Society of Architectural Historians* 27 (May 1968): 140–46.

Andrews, Alfred. "Gideon Shryock — Kentucky Architect and the Greek Revival Architecture in Kentucky." *The Filson Club Quarterly* 56 (Autumn 1944): 67–77.

Ashton, Eugene. "The Latrobe Corn-Stalk Columns." *The Magazine of American History* 18 (August 1887): 126–29.

Attebery, Jennifer Eastman. "The Square Cabin: A Folk House Type in Idaho." *Idaho Yesterdays* 26 (September 1982): 25–31.

Bernstein, Richard. "Unsettling the Old West." *New York Times Magazine* (18 March 1990): 34–35, 56–57, 59.

Brown, Elizabeth Esson. "History of the Brown House." *Marion County History* 1 (1955): 6–9.

Buck, Mrs. W. W. "Reminiscences." *Oregon Pioneer Association Transactions* 21 (1891): 67–69, hereafter cited as *OPAT*.

Burnett, Peter H. "Recollections and Opinions of an Old Pioneer." Oregon *Historical Quarterly* 5 (December 1904): 272–305, hereafter cited as *OHQ*.

"Colver House Receives Marker." *Table Rock Sentinel, Newsletter of the Southern Oregon Historical Society* 1 (March 1981): 4.

Davis, W. N., Jr. "Will the West Survive as a Field in American History? A Survey Report." *Mississippi Valley Historical Review* 50 (March 1964): 672–85.

Dole, Philip. "The Calef Farm: Region and Style in Oregon." *Journal of the Society of Architectural Historians* 23 (December 1964): 201–9.

———. "Farmhouses and Barns in Early Lane County." *Lane County Historian* 10 (August 1965): 28–37.

Douglas, Jesse S. "Origins of the Population of Oregon, 1850." *Pacific Northwest Historical Quarterly* 41 (April 1950): 93–110.

Dye, Eva Emery. "Women's Part in the Drama of the Northwest." *OPAT* 21 (1894): 42–46.

Earle, Edward M. "American Interest in the Greek Cause, 1821–1827." *American Historical Review* 33 (October 1927): 44–63.

Eells, Myron. "Mrs. Mary Richardson Walker." *OPAT* 24 (1897): 140–41.

Everett, Edward, ed. "Anastasius; or the Memoirs of a Greek." *North American Review* 11 (October 1820): 275–89.

Fitz-Gibbon, Costen. "Latrobe and the Centre Square Pump House." *Architectural Record* 52 (July 1927): 19–22.

Garth, Thomas R., Jr. "Early Architecture in the Northwest." *Pacific Northwest Quarterly* 38 (January 1947): 215–32.

Gilchrist, Agnes Addison. "Latrobe vs. Strickland." *Journal of the Society of Architectural Historians* 2 (July 1942): 26–29.

Bibliography

Gilman, Arthur. *North American Review* 58 (April 1844): 440–63.

Glassie, Henry. "Eighteenth-Century Cultural Process in Delaware Valley Folk Building." *Winterthur Portfolio* 7 (Autumn 1972): 29–57.

Hamlin, Talbot. "Benjamin Henry Latrobe: The Man and the Architect." *The Maryland Historical Magazine* 38 (January 1943): 39–60.

———. "Some Greek Revival Architects of Philadelphia." *Pennsylvania Magazine of History and Biography* 65 (April 1941): 121–44.

Hammond, Bray. "The Second Bank of the United States." *Transactions of the American Philosophical Society* 43 (March 1953): 80–85.

Handlin, David P. "New England Architects in New York, 1820–1840." *American Quarterly* 19 (Winter 1967): 681–95.

Harrington, J. C. "Archeology as an Auxiliary to American History." *American Anthropologist* 57 (December 1955): 1120–30.

"History of Oregon." *OPAT* 15 (1888): 46–98.

Jackson, W. Turrentine. "A Brief Message for the Young and/or Ambitious: Comparative Frontiers as a Field of Investigation." *Western Historical Quarterly* 9 (1978): 5–18.

"James Duval Holman." *OPAT* 21 (1894): 45.

Johansen, Dorothy O. "Oregon Steam Navigation Company: An Example of Capitalism on the Frontier." *Pacific Historical Review* 10 (June 1941): 179–88.

———. "A Working Hypothesis for the Study of Migrations." *Pacific Historical Review* 36 (February 1967): 4–19.

Kimball, Fiske. "The Bank of Pennsylvania, an Unknown Masterpiece of American Classicism." *Architectural Record* 43 (August 1918): 132–39.

———. "The Bank of the United States, 1818–1824." *Architectural Record* 58 (December 1925): 581–94.

Kirker, Harold. "California Architecture and Its Relation to Contemporary Trends in Europe and America." *California Historical Quarterly* 51 (March 1972): 289–305.

Kniffen, Fred B. "Folk Housing: Key to Diffusion." *Annals of the Association of American Geographers* 55 (December 1965): 549–77.

———. "Louisiana House Types." *Annals of the Association of American Geographers* 26 (1936): 179–93.

———, and Henry Glassie. "Building in Wood in the Eastern United States: A Time-Space Perspective." *Geographical Review* 66 (March 1966): 40–66.

Koreas, A., ed. "The Ethics of Aristotle." Translated and reviewed by Edward Everett. *North American Review* 17 (October 1823): 415–20.

Lancaster, Clay. "Gideon Shryock and John McMurtry: Architect and Builder in Kentucky." *The Art Quarterly* 56 (Autumn 1943): 257–75.

———. "Greek Revival Architecture in Alabama." *Alabama Architecture* 5 (January–February 1969): 1–15.

Lyman, H. S. "Reminiscences of Hugh Cosgrove." *OHQ* 1 (June 1900): 246–66.

———. "Reminiscences of William M. Case." *OHQ* 1 (September 1900): 267–95.

McArthur, Harriet K. "A Biographical Sketch of Hon. J. W. Nesmith." *OPAT* 13 (1886): 30–36.

Mahoney, Nell Savage. "William Strickland and the Building of Tennessee's Capitol, 1845–1854." *Tennessee Historical Quarterly* 4 (July 1945): 99–153.

Majors, Howard. "The Greek Revival: American National Expression." *The Architectural Forum* 40 (February 1924): 45–110.

Malone, Michael P., and Rodman W. Paul. "Tradition and Challenge in Western Historiography." *Western Historical Quarterly* 16 (1985): 27–53.

Minto, John. "Reminiscences of Experiences on the Oregon Trail in 1844." *OHQ* 2 (September 1901): 121–254.

———. "Robert Wilson Morrison." *OPAT* 21 (1894): 61.

Moore, Saundra. "Oregon's First Capitols, 1853–1876." *Marion County History* 5 (1959): 13–16.

Nedry, H. S., ed. "Willamette Valley in 1859: The Diary of a Tour." *OHQ* 46 (September 1945): 239–54.

Paul, Rodman W. "The Mormons as a Theme in Western Historical Writing." *Journal of American History* 54 (December 1967): 511–23.

Pomeroy, Earl. "Toward a Reorientation of Western History: Continuity and Environment." *Mississippi Valley Historical Review* 41 (March 1955): 579–600.

Prown, Jules. "Style as Evidence." *Winterthur Portfolio* 15 (Autumn 1980): 197–210.

Ross, Marion Dean. "Architecture in Oregon, 1845–1895." *OHQ* 57 (March 1956): 1–47.

Rydell, Robert W., ed. "Architecture and the American West." (A Special Issue) *Pacific Historical Review* 54 (November 1985): 397–513.

Schlereth, Thomas J., ed. *American Quarterly* 35 (1983): 236–338.

Upton, Dell. "Pattern Books and Professionalism: Aspects of the Transformation of Domestic Architecture in America, 1800–1860." *Winterthur Portfolio* 19 (Autumn 1984): 107–50.

"The Vermont State House." *American Magazine of Useful Knowledge* 3 (1836): 205–10.

"William Bybee: Land Baron." *Table Rock Sentinel, Newsletter of the Southern Oregon Historical Society* 1 (July 1981): 3–5.

Winslow, Walter C. "Contests Over the State Capital of Oregon." *OHQ* 9 (June 1908): 173–78.

Winter, Robert. "Architecture on the Frontier: The Mormon Experiment." *Pacific Historical Review* 43 (March 1974): 50–60.

Young, F. G. "Financial History of Oregon, 1849–1859." *OHQ* 8 (March 1907): 101–51.

BOOKS

Aberdeen, George Hamilton. *An Inquiry into the Principles of Beauty in Grecian Architecture: With an Historical View.* London: John Weale, 1960.

Andrews, Wayne. *Architecture, Ambition and Americans: A Social History of American Architecture.* New York: Free Press, 1978.

Bancroft, Hubert Howe. *The History of Oregon.* 2 vols. San Francisco: History Company, 1888.

Bassett, John, ed. *Correspondence of Andrew Jackson.* 7 vols. Washington, D.C.: Carnegie Institute, 1927–35.

Benjamin, Asher. *The American Builder's Companion.* Boston: Etheridge and Bliss, 1806.

———. *American Builder's Companion,* 6th ed. Boston: R. P. and C. Williams, 1826; reprint ed. New York: Dover Publications, Inc., 1969.

———. *The Builder's Guide.* Boston: Perkins and Marvin, 1839.

———. *The Country Builder's Assistant.* Greenfield, Mass.: Thomas Dickman, 1797.

———. *The Elements of Architecture.* Boston: B. B. Massey, 1843.

———. *The Practical House Carpenter.* Boston: R. P. and C. Williams, and Ammin and Smith, 1830.

———. *The Practice of Architecture.* Boston: Benjamin, Carter, Hendie and Company, 1833.

———. *The Rudiments of Architecture.* Boston: Munroe and Francis, 1814.

Bibber, Joyce K. *A Home for Everyone: The Greek Revival and Maine Domestic Architecture.* Lanham, Md.: AASLH Press, 1989.

Bonta, Juan Pablo. *Architecture and Its Interpretations.* Cambridge, Mass.: MIT Press, 1986.

Bowen, William. *Willamette Valley: Migration and Settlement on the Oregon Frontier.* Seattle: University of Washington Press, 1978.

Brunvand, Jan H., ed. *The Study of American Folklore.* New York: W. W. Norton and Company, 1968.

Bryan, John M., ed. *Robert Mills: Architect.* Washington, D.C.: AIA Press, 1989.

Burnham, Smith, comp. *The First National Bank of West Chester of Chester County, Pennsylvania: 1814–1914.* n.p.: n.d.

Caley, George L. *Footprints of the Past.* Smyrna, Del.: Shane Quality Press, 1978.

Carter, Edward C., II. *The Virginia Journals of Benjamin Henry Latrobe, 1795–1798.* 2 vols. New Haven, Conn.: Yale University Press, 1977.

Carter, Thomas, and Bernard Herman. *Perspectives in Vernacular Architecture.* 3 vols. Columbia: University of Missouri Press, 1989.

Christovich, Mary Louise, et al., eds. *New Orleans Architecture.* 6 vols. Gretna La.: Pelican Publishing Company, 1974–80.

Cochran, Gifford A. *Grandeur in Tennessee: Classical Revival Architecture in a Pioneer State.* New York: J. J. Augustin, 1946.

Coulton, J. J. *Ancient Greek Architects at Work: Problems of Structure and Design.* Ithaca, N.Y.: Cornell University Press, 1977.

Crook, J. Mordaunt. *The Dilemma of Style: Architectural Ideals from the Picturesque to the Post-Modern.* Chicago: University of Chicago Press, 1987.

Dickens, Charles. *American Notes.* Edited by Michael Slater. Austin: University of Texas Press, 1978.

di Valmarana, Mario, ed. *Building by the Book.* 2 vols. Charlottesville: University of Virginia Press, 1986.

Dodds, Gordon B. *Oregon: A Bicentennial History.* New York: W. W. Norton and Company, 1977.

Douglass, Frederick. *My Bondage and My Freedom.* New York: Miller, Orton, and Mulligan, 1855.

Downing, Andrew Jackson. *The Architecture of Country Houses.* New York: D. Appleton and Company, 1850; reprint ed. New York: Dover Publications, Inc., 1969.

Downing, Antoinette Forrester. *Early Houses of Rhode Island.* Richmond, Va.: Garrett and Massie, 1937.

Drury, Clifford. *Marcus and Narcissa Whitman and the Opening of Old Oregon.* 2 vols. Glendale, Calif.: Arthur H. Clark Company, 1973.

———. *Nine Years with the Spokane Indians: The Diary, 1838–1848, of Elkanah Walker.* Glendale, Calif.: Arthur H. Clark Company, 1976.

Dunbar, Seymour. *A History of Travel in America.* New York: Tudor Publishing Company, 1937.

Eliot, William Havard. *A Description of the Tremont House with Architectural Illustrations.* Boston: Gray and Bowen, 1830.

Faragher, John Mack. *Women and Men on the Overland Trail.* New Haven, Conn.: Yale University Press, 1979.

Ferguson, Leland, ed. *Historical Archeology and the Importance of Material Things.* New York: Chelsea House Publishers, 1968.

Festschrift: A Collection of Essays in Architectural History Dedicated to Marion Dean Ross on His 65th Birthday. Portland: Society of Architectural Historians, Northern Pacific Chapter, 1979.

Frary, I. T. *Early Houses of Ohio.* Richmond, Va.: Garrett and Massey, 1936.

Gallagher, H. M. Pierce. *Robert Mills: Architect of the Washington Monument.* New York: Columbia University Press, 1935.

Genealogical Material in Oregon Donation Land Claims Abstracted from Applications. 3 vols. Portland: Genealogical Forum of Portland, 1962.

Gilchrist, Agnes Addison. *William Strickland, Architect and Engineer: 1788–1854.* Philadelphia: University of Pennsylvania Press, 1950.

Glassie, Henry. *Folk Housing in Middle Virginia: A Structural Analysis of Historical Artifacts.* Knoxville: University of Tennessee Press, 1975.

———. *Patterns in the Material Folk Culture of the Eastern United States.* Philadelphia: University of Pennsylvania Press, 1968.

Goetzmann, William. *Exploration and Empire: The Explorer and the Scientist in the Winning of the American West*. New York: Alfred A. Knopf, Inc., 1966.

The Greek Revival in the United States. New York: Metropolitan Museum of Art, 1943.

Gressley, Gene M., ed. *The American West: A Reorientation*. University of Wyoming Publications 32. Laramie: University of Wyoming Press, 1966.

Gunn, Giles B.. *The Culture of Criticism and the Criticism of Culture*. New York: Oxford University Press, 1987.

Hafen, Leroy, and Ann W. Hafen, eds. *To the Rockies and Oregon, 1839–1842*. 3 vols. Glendale, Calif.: Arthur H. Clark Company, 1955.

Hale, Roger Newton. *Town and Davis, Architects: Pioneers in American Revivalist Architecture*. New York: Columbia University Press, 1942.

Hamlin, Talbot. *Benjamin Henry Latrobe*. New York: Oxford University Press, 1955.

————. *Greek Revival Architecture in America: Being an Account of Important Trends in American Architecture and American Life Prior to the War Between the States*. New York: Oxford University Press, 1944.

Hammond, Bray. *Banks and Politics in America, From the Revolution to the Civil War*. Princeton, N.J.: Princeton University Press, 1957.

Handlin, David. *The American Home: Architecture and Society, 1815–1915*. Boston: Little, Brown and Company, 1979.

Hatfield, H. C., *Winkelmann and his German Critics, 1755–1781: A Prelude to the Classical Age*. New York: King's Crown Press, 1843.

Haviland, John, and Hugh Beaufort. *The Builder's Assistant*. 3 vols. Philadelphia: John Bloren, 1818–21.

Herman, Bernard. *Architecture and Rural Life in Central Delaware*. Knoxville: University of Tennessee Press, 1987.

Hines, Gustavus. *Oregon and Its Institutions*. New York: Carlton and Porter, 1868.

Hines, H. K. *An Illustrated History of the State of Oregon*. Chicago: Lewis Publishing Co., 1893.

Hitchcock, Henry-Russell, and William Seale. *Temples of Democracy: The State Capitols of the USA*. New York: Harcourt, Brace, and Jovanovich, 1976.

Holliday, J. S. *The World Rushed In: The California Gold Rush Experience*. New York: Simon and Shuster, 1981.

Hume, Ivor Noel. *Historical Archeology*. New York: Alfred A. Knopf, Inc., 1969.

Hussey, John. *A History of Fort Vancouver and Its Physical Plan*. Tacoma: Washington State Historical Society, 1957.

James, Marquis. *The Life of Andrew Jackson*. New York: Garden City Publishing Company, 1938.

Johansen, Dorothy O., and Charles M. Gates. *Empire of the Columbia: A History of the Pacific Northwest*. 2d ed. New York: Harper and Row, Publishers, 1967.

202

Bibliography

Johnston, Frances Benjamin, and Thomas Tileston Waterman. *The Early Architecture of North Carolina*. Chapel Hill: University of North Carolina Press, 1941.

Kennedy, Roger G. *Greek Revival America*. New York: Stewart, Tabori, and Chang, 1989.

Kirker, Harold. *California's Architectural Frontier: Style and Tradition in the Nineteenth Century*. San Marino, Calif.: Huntington Library, 1960; reprint ed. Salt Lake City: University of Utah Press, 1973.

Kostof, Spiro. *A History of Architecture: Settings and Rituals*. New York: Oxford University Press, 1985.

Lafever, Minard. *The Beauties of Modern Architecture*. New York: D. Appleton and Company, 1835; reprint ed. New York: De Capo Press, 1968.

———. *The Modern Builder's Guide*. New York: Collins and Hanney, 1833.

———. *The Young Builder's General Instructor*. Newark, N.J.: W. Tuttle and Company, 1829.

Lancaster, Clay. *The Architecture of Historic Nantucket*. New York: McGraw-Hill, 1972.

Lang, Berel. *The Concept of Style*. Philadelphia: University of Pennsylvania Press, 1979.

Lang, H. O., ed. *History of the Willamette Valley*. Portland: Hines and Lang, 1885.

Larkin, Oliver W. *Art and Life in America*. New York: Holt, Rinehart, and Winston, 1960.

Latrobe, Benjamin Henry. *The Journals of Latrobe: Being Notes and Sketches of an Architect, Naturalist, and Traveler in the United States from 1796 to 1820*. New York: D. Appleton and Company, 1905.

Lavender, David S. *Land of Giants: The Drive in the Pacific Northwest, 1750–1950*. Garden City, N.Y.: Doubleday, 1958.

Levasseur, August. *Lafayette in America: 1824–1825*. 2 vols. Philadelphia: Carey, Lea, and Carey, 1829.

Limerick, Patricia Nelson. *The Legacy of Conquest: The Unbroken Past of the American West*. New York: W. W. Norton and Company, 1987.

Liscombe, Rhodri Windsor. *The Church Architecture of Robert Mills*. Easley, S.C.: Southern Historical Press, 1985.

McMurry, Sally. *Families and Farmhouses in 19th Century America*. New York: Oxford University Press, 1988.

Maine Catalogue: A List of Measured Drawings, Photographs, and Written Documents in the Historical American Building Survey. Augusta: Maine State Museum, 1974.

Malone, Michael, ed. *Historians and the American West*. Lincoln: University of Nebraska Press, 1983.

Marshall, Howard Wright. *Folk Architecture in Little Dixie: A Regional Culture in Missouri*. Columbia: University of Missouri Press, 1981.

Bibliography

Meidell, Pamela S., ed. *Oregon Style: Architecture from 1840 to the 1950s*. Portland: Professional Book Center, Inc., 1983.

Mills, Randall V. *Stern-Wheelers Up Columbia: A Century of Steamboating in the Oregon Country*. Palo Alto, Calif.: Pacific Books, 1947; reprint ed. Lincoln: University of Nebraska Press, 1977.

Myres, Sandra L. *Westering Women and the Frontier Experience, 1800–1915*. Albuquerque: University of New Mexico Press, 1982.

Nelligan, Murray H. *Lee Mansion: National Memorial*. U.S. Department of the Interior. National Park Service Historical Series #6. Washington, D.C.: Government Printing Office, n.d.

Nichols, Frederick Doveton. *Thomas Jefferson's Architectural Drawings*. Boston: Massachusetts Historical Society, 1961.

Nye, Mary Greene. *Vermont's State House*. Montpelier: Vermont Publicity Service, 1936.

O'Donnell, Terrence, and Thomas Vaughan. *Portland: A Historical Sketch and Guide*. Portland: Oregon Historical Society, 1976.

Paul, Rodman W. *Mining Frontiers of the Far West, 1848–1880*. New York: Holt, Rinehart, and Winston, 1963.

Pierson, William H., Jr. *American Buildings and Their Architects: The Colonial and Neoclassical Styles*. Garden City, N.Y.: Doubleday and Company, Inc., 1970.

Pomeroy, Earl. *The Pacific Slope: A History of California, Oregon, Washington, Idaho, Utah, and Nevada*. New York: Alfred A. Knopf, Inc., 1965.

Portland, Multnomah County, Oregon. San Francisco: Kuchel and Dresel, 1858.

Quimby, M. G., ed. *Material Culture and the Study of American Life*. New York: W. W. Norton and Company, 1978.

Ross, Marion Dean. *A Century of Architecture in Oregon, 1859–1959*. Portland: Oregon Chapter of the American Institute of Architects, 1959.

Schlereth, Thomas J. *Artifacts and the American Past*. Nashville: AASLH Press, 1980.

———. *Material Culture Studies in America*. Nashville: AASLH Press, 1982.

Schmidt, Carl F. *Greek Revival Architecture in the Rochester [New York] Area*. Scottsdale, N.Y.: Carl F. Schmidt, 1946.

Scott, Harvey W. *History of the Oregon Country*. 2 vols. Cambridge: Riverside Press, 1924.

Scott, Mary Wingfield. *Houses of Old Richmond*. Richmond, Va.: Valentine Museum, n.d.

Shaw, Edward. *Rural Architecture*. Boston: James B. Dow, 1843.

Steffen, Jerome O. *Comparative Frontiers: A Proposal for Studying the American West*. Norman: University of Oklahoma Press, 1980.

Stuart, James, and Nicolas Revett. *The Antiquities of Athens*. 4 vols. London: J. Haberkorn, 1762–1816.

Teitelman, Edward, and Richard W. Longstreth. *Architecture in Philadelphia: A Guide*. Cambridge, Mass.: MIT Press, 1981.

Throckmorton, Arthur L. *Oregon Argonauts: Merchant Adventurers on the Western Frontier.* Portland: Oregon Historical Society, 1961.

Trollope, Frances M. *Domestic Manners of the Americans.* London: Whitaker, Trecher, and Company, 1832.

Unruh, John D., Jr. *The Plains Across: The Overland Emigrants and the Trans-Mississippi West, 1840–1860.* Urbana: University of Illinois Press, 1979.

Upton, Dell, and Michael Vlach. *Common Places: Readings in American Vernacular Architecture.* Athens: University of Georgia Press, 1986.

Vaughan, Thomas. *The Bybee-Howell House on Sauvie Island.* Portland: Oregon Historical Society, 1974.

——, and George McMath. *A Century of Portland Architecture.* Portland: Oregon Historical Society, 1967.

——, and Virginia Guest Ferriday, eds. *Space, Style, and Structure: Building in Northwest America.* 2 vols. Portland: Oregon Historical Society, 1974.

Wadkin, David. *The Rise of Architectural History.* London: Architectural Press, 1981.

Walling, A. G. *An Illustrated History of Lane County, Oregon.* Portland: Western Publishing Company, 1884.

Weatherford, Mark V. *The Sperry-Weatherford Family.* Albany, Oreg.: n.p., 1960.

Wells, Camille. *Perspectives in Vernacular Architecture II.* Columbia: University of Missouri Press, 1986.

Wheildon, William. *Memoir of Solomon Willard.* Boston: Monument Association, 1865.

Whiffen, Marcus. *American Architecture Since 1780: A Guide to the Styles.* Cambridge, Mass.: MIT Press, 1969.

Wiebenson, Dora. *Sources of Greek Revival Architecture.* London: A. Zwemmer, Ltd., 1969.

Works Progress Administration. Federal Writers Project of Ohio. *Chillicothe and Ross Counties.* Chillicothe: Ross County Northwest Territory Committee, 1938.

Wright, Gwendolen. *Moralism and the Model Home.* Chicago: University of Chicago Press, 1980.

UNPUBLISHED ITEMS

Palmer, Joel. "Diaries of Joel Palmer." 1860. Typescript manuscript. Oregon State Library. Salem.

Swinney, Sonja. "The House of Many Faces [Sam Colver House]." Unpublished research paper. Southern Oregon Historical Society. Jacksonville, 1960.

"William Case, 1820–1903, Champoeg, Oregon." Typed manuscript, n.d. National Register nomination file. Oregon State Parks and Recreation Division. Department of Transportation. Salem.

INDEX